P9-CKR-409

WEATHER FORCE

WEATHER FORCE

CLIMATE AND ITS IMPACT ON OUR WORLD
JOHN GRIBBIN

G.P. PUTNAM'S SONS NEW YORK

A BISON BOOK

Published by
G. P. Putnam's Sons
200 Madison Avenue
New York, NY 10016
USA

Copyright © 1979
Bison Books Limited

Produced by
Bison Books Limited
4 Cromwell Place
London SW7

Library of Congress Catalog
Card number 79-51033

ISBN 399-12400-4

Printed in Hong Kong

Editor: John Man
Designer: Laurence Bradbury

CONTENTS

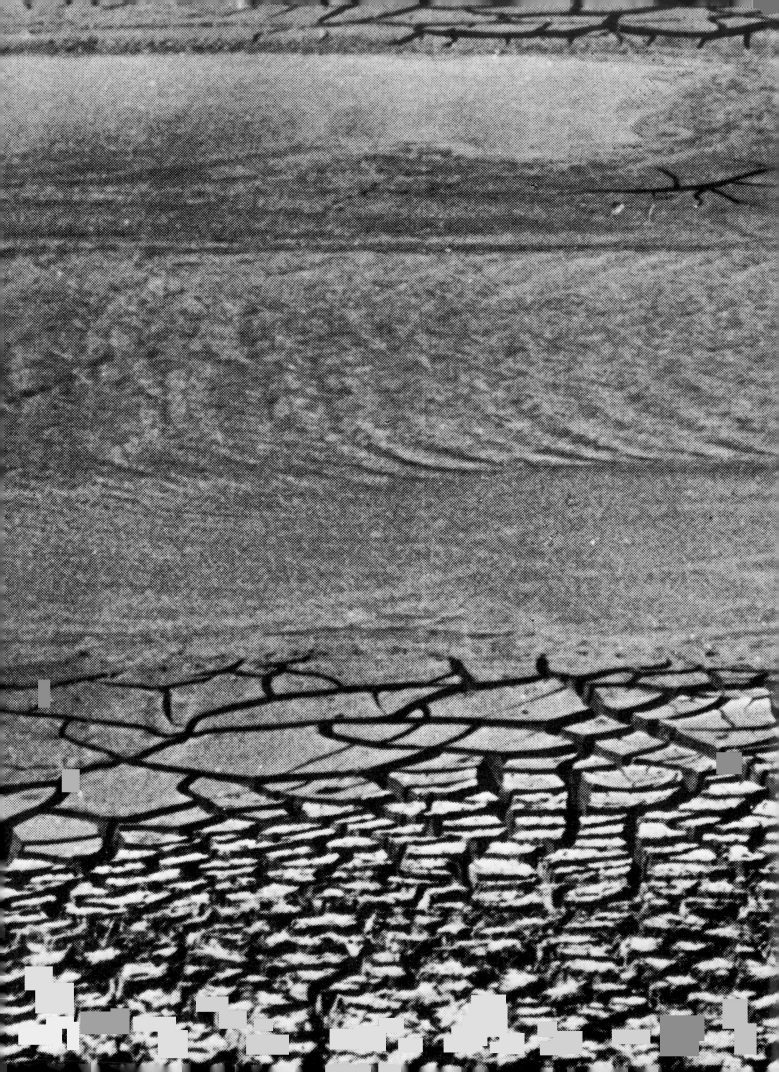

1: THE BIG HEAT - THE BIG FREEZE

The 1970s have seen extreme weather conditions strike across the world. In particular, the US and Britain have been frozen and scorched by the worst conditions in many decades. This chapter recalls that extraordinary sequence of climatic events.

In 1978 the European Economic Community initiated a major study of climatic change and the way extremes of weather can disrupt our lives. In announcing the decision, the EEC drew attention to a remarkable sequence of extremes. In the preceding fifteen years Europe had suffered:
—the coldest winter since 1740;
—the driest winter since 1743;
—the mildest winter since 1834;
—the greatest drought since 1726;
—the hottest month (July 1976) since records began 300 years ago.

Over the same few years a similar pattern had been seen across the world—California, New York, Africa, India, the Soviet Union and in many other areas. Everywhere there was just one predictable theme to the story: unpredictability. The weather had become violent and variable, with extremes unlike anything in living memory occurring almost routinely.

That pattern is still with us. Hard on the heels of the EEC report came another season for the European record books: over much of Europe and southern England, the autumn of 1978 turned into a scorcher, mocking the cold and rain of the 'summer' months just past and giving the headline writers more excuses for superlatives. But now we know why these seemingly bizarre events are taking place. It is not that the weather we are getting now—and have had for the past decade and a half—is unusual. Rather, it seems that the rest of 'living memory' spanned an unusual time, a series of decades extraordinarily bland compared with the forceful weather of previous (and probably future) conditions. Much of this book will be concerned with pointing out and explaining the causes of this pattern. But first it is as well to look at some of the extreme weather conditions of the 1970s, to recall the feel of conditions we may well have to regard as normal in future.

Although many areas of the world suffered droughts in the mid-1970s, pride of place in any historical review must go to the great California drought of 1976–77, the worst in the US since the days of the notorious dust-bowl of the 1930s. The effect on agriculture in particular was disastrous. California provides 25 percent of all US food, including 40 percent of the vegetables, 60 percent of the fruit and a full 90 percent of some crops, including tomatoes. Agriculture is California's leading

industry and was bringing in $9000 million in 1975, the year before the drought set in. By February 1976 cattle were already being slaughtered before they actually starved to death in the dry pastures. Beef prices fell temporarily as a surplus hit on the market, then rose precipitously as scarcity set in. At this time the drought was already being called the worst in living memory—and there was more than a year of it still to come. Drought losses in 1977 amounted to some $5000 million.

But not only agriculture was affected. The lack of snow on the mountains hit the tourist industry of California and many other western states—Oregon, Washington, Nevada, Colorado, Montana and Wyoming (although these received less publicity simply because they do not have such large populations).

Over in Europe—or, at least, parts of Europe—a counterpart to the great California drought had started a year earlier, in 1975, so that it was the summer of 1976, rather than 1977, which goes down in the memory of many Europeans as the time of great drought. In England no one could have reasonably expected 1975—the fifth driest year of the 20th century—to be followed by another dry summer, let alone the unremitting desiccation that actually occurred. By the end of July reservoirs in the western counties of Devon and Cornwall were down to 23 percent capacity; the River Thames itself dried up completely for nine miles at its source; and by the autumn stand-pipes dispensing rationed quantities of water became common sights in the streets of western and southern Britain.

The hottest June of the century brought blushes to the faces of official forecasters at the UK Meteorological Office, who failed to predict the heatwave. Beer sales boomed, as did the business at holiday resorts, but once again the farmers suffered. By the autumn the meteorological men were blushing again; having failed to predict the drought, they also failed to predict its end—a dramatic end when the months without rain were broken by epic downpours. The driest 16-month period in the meteorological records of England and Wales was followed by the second wettest September–October since records began. This pleased the farmers at first, who saw some of their crops recovering dramatically, due to the life-giving water. Their delight was short-lived: their

In Wales's Taf Fechan Reservoir, in August 1976, an official points out drought effects.

An English beer-tanker switches roles to bring water to thirsty sheep.

once-arid pastures turned green, only to disappear under water. Machinery, dragged on to the soggy land to harvest their produce, bogged down.

The cracked reservoirs took some time to fill up too so that in parts of the West Country water remained rationed, and had to be collected from the stand-pipes by local residents well wrapped up against the teeming rain. A headline in *The Times* on 4 January 1977 summed it all up: 'Sun, Drought, Wind, Rain made 1976 a Year of Climatic Extremes.'

The extremes—and the changes—were truly extraordinary, as a summary of events world-wide shows. At the same time as the drought in England and Wales, Scotland had ample rain, while just to the east, around the Baltic Sea, a surfeit of rain was bringing its problems for the Soviet grain farmers. Alternating bands of drought and excess precipitation stepped around the globe from California (dry) through the eastern US (wet) to southern Europe (dry), Russia (wet) and China (dry), where soil moisture was measured at 60 percent of normal in March and harvests failed dramatically.

At the beginning of 1978, four weeks' torrential rain and snow after the drought meant 'disaster' for Californians. On the night of 24 September 1976 storms hit Cornwall; floods rushed through the town of Polperro and carried a man aged 85 out of the window of his house to his death. In early August 1978, for example, torrential rain and snow (in *August!*) blocked mountain passes in the Swiss and Italian Alps. Fourteen people were killed, including an 18-year-old Swiss student drowned at a camp site on the banks of the Ticino river, a 55-year-old man who was standing on a bridge which collapsed under him and two 12-year-old girls who were swept away by a landslide. These events can be seen as part of a pattern of oscillations in a great river of air in the upper atmosphere, the jet stream (see Chapter 2). When the pattern changed, extreme followed extreme around the world.

Such freak disasters are automatically associated with tragedy and death. But *any* extreme involves suffering, even if the cost in terms of human life cannot be counted immediately. Who appreciated at the time that the English summer of 1976, so pleasant for vacationers, brought its own toll of death? In the southeast of England the average toll of 1780 deaths in the week ending 25 June rose in the heatwave of the following week by 28 percent, to 2286. In all likelihood, the heatwave was primarily responsible for the death of 500 people in this one week and in this one area. This vastly greater 'disaster' caused no sensation at the time, however, appearing only in the statistics when these were gathered at a later date.

In greater London the effect was even more pronounced as the heatwave was added to the other hazards of city life. There, the increase in mortality over the same two weeks was 33 percent, from 1475 to 1956. The old, of course, were hardest hit, with graphs of weekly average temperature and deaths of the population of over 65 running almost uncannily in step. Usually most deaths occur in the harsher days of winter. But the summer of 1976 proved almost as harsh as winter: the peak

Dead fish clog an English stream, sluggish and increasingly stagnant from the drought.

figures of late June–early July were unmatched in any week until December.

The East suffered its share of weather 'freaks' in the 1970s, although to many people in the developed world, news of droughts, floods or famine from the Third World is regarded as hardly 'news' at all. What is a disaster where deaths from hunger are commonplace? News of disasters of a different sort strikes home only when it is abundantly clear that millions of people are suffering something worse than usual. For the same reason, all too often aid from the rich countries arrives only after the worst of the disaster is past. An event like the flood disaster that hit India in September 1978, however, is immediate to even the most cynical.

Late rains swept in at the tail end of the monsoon season, bringing the worst floods for 100 years. In New Delhi four million people were cut off. In Calcutta, on the coast at the mouth of the Ganges, the situation was equally bad. Road and rail links were destroyed and crops washed away. Eyewitnesses reported hundreds of bodies floating in the swollen rivers, with official estimates recording upwards of 15,000 dead. Between the two great cities, the northern states of Uttar Pradesh, Haryana and the Punjab, and northern districts of West Bengal were all hard hit by flooding. Overall, the disaster was the worst ever to hit India (with the exception of the Andhra Pradesh cyclone of 1977—of which more later). Early estimates of the cost, apart from the terrible loss of life, approached £100 ($200) million, with about 5 percent of the entire population of India directly affected by the floods and well over half a million houses destroyed or seriously damaged. Government figures put it in cold statistics—46,166 villages affected over an area of 21.7 million acres and 12.9 million acres of crops destroyed.

The aftermath of this disaster remains. Flood victims, deprived of housing and livelihood, have to rebuild their lives or become more statistics on the ledgers of refugee camps; the government, hardly the wealthiest in the world, is committed to a £500 million ($1 billion) program of flood control measures over the next five years. But will even this be enough? Does the worst flooding for a hundred years mean a further century's respite, or does it herald a succession of violent acts from the weather outside the run of what we are used to thinking of as 'normal'?

Looking once again at the so-called 'temperate' countries of higher latitudes, it looks increasingly likely that there really has been a change for the worse, bringing more violent extremes of weather and, perhaps, presaging still more violence to come. Take the Big Freezes of 1976–78: in 1977–78 even bland old Britain got hit by the frosts. In January ferocious snow storms brought Scotland to a frozen standstill for several days. A few weeks later the West Country—the region worst hit by drought only 18 months before—disappeared under the snow, while strong winds and flooding brought their own troubles to the east coast.

It is the two Arctic winters that hit the eastern United States in 1976–77 and 1977–78 that will be remembered as something really dramatic. And, just possibly, those severe winters, combined with the severe droughts farther west, will be seen to have finally convinced governments and civil servants that the weather will remain a force to be reckoned with.

Yet again the phrase that had become so familiar in weather reports in the 1970s was used to describe the US winter of 1976–77 – 'the worst for a hundred years.' At the end of January 1977 the most sophisticated economy in the world learned first-hand of the power of the weather. Motorists trapped in their cars by blizzards suffocated. More than half a million workers were laid off in New Jersey alone, in no small measure because the run-down gas supply system proved inadequate to cope with the demands of industry and the public in such severe weather conditions. By 30 January the Commerce Department in Washington estimated that the temporarily unemployed nationwide amounted to over 1.6 million.

In Buffalo, perhaps the worst-hit center, well over 12 feet (3.6 m) of snow by the end of January—compared with the usual $3\frac{1}{2}$ to 4 feet (1 to 1.2 m)—closed the airport and

In 1976 while Britain sweltered, Moscow was drenched by rains that brought flash floods, like the one shown here.

made streets almost impassable to ordinary traffic, including police vehicles. Inevitably looters took advantage of the situation, hitting shops, businesses, private homes and stalled cars abandoned in the snow. But even the looters could not get out during the worst day, Friday 28 January, when 4 inches (10 cm) of snow fell in a 17½ hour period, with a driving 68 mph (109 kph) wind blasting it on its way.

By mid-February the US Weather Service declared officially that the winter for the eastern two-thirds of the country was the coldest since the founding of the Republic. Frost bit down even into Florida, where temperatures of 17°F (–8°C) wiped out more than 10 percent of the citrus crop in a few hours; snow fell in Miami, while to the north Lake Erie froze solid.

Within weeks of the coming of spring, however, the winter of 1977 was nothing more than a memory to most people, the stuff of folk-lore. Few took any real notice of those climatologists (myself included) who warned that this 'worst winter for a hundred years' might be setting the new pattern of weather to come. It was only when the next winter, 1977–78, brought *even worse* conditions than the remarkable winter of 1977 that people began to sit up and take notice.

There are numerous accounts of the impact of that winter. The one that had the greatest effect on me was a personal comment by a friend, who wrote to me in late February 1978 from Brockton, Massachusetts. A few weeks before, I had sent him a copy of my then latest book (*Forecasts, Famines and Freezes*) warning of more dire winters for the eastern US. He replied as follows:

'I've been meaning to write you and thank you for the copy of the book on weather which you sent me, but I've been rather busy shovelling snow. Shortly after your book arrived, this area was hit with 21 inches of snow in 24 hours, the most since they started keeping records in Boston over 100 years ago for a 24-hour period. It hit on a Friday, giving some time for snow clearance over the weekend, but things were pretty much a mess the following week in a city dependent on commuter traffic. It was dubbed "Superstorm '78" and all the newspapers put out special sections commemorating this historic storm. Three

In February 1977 cars in a Buffalo, NY, parking lot lie buried in the worst snows in living memory.

weeks later, a second storm dropped 27 inches (69 cm) in 24 hours on Boston (more than that to the south, where I live) in a storm accompanied by winds up to 100 mph (160 kph) in what was called a "snow hurricane." It was the worst snowstorm in 90 years, and will certainly be known as the Blizzard of '78. Three thousand cars were stranded on the highways surrounding Boston, as the storm hit just after noon and caught the people who left Boston in the late afternoon, expecting to get home through the snow like they always had before. A state of emergency was declared by the State's Governor and lasted for 46 days, with all private cars barred from the roads and businesses closed. Personally, I had a great time skiing all over this city of 100,000 people that I live in; but people on the coast were badly battered, as the storm was at its peak during a high tide on the night of a new moon. Anyway, your prediction that last winter was no fluke has been borne out. And some people are picking up

on the idea that the weather is not getting hotter or colder, but just more variable.

'One thing it showed was how dependent Boston is on the automobile. The last really bad winter was 30 years ago; and at that time, most people lived within the city and few had cars. Now everybody lives out in the suburbs and drives to work, and those in the city have cars parked on the street, complicating the snow plowing job. Also, it turns out that one of the agencies responsible for snow plowing can only really handle a 6-inch (15-cm) storm. That I consider ludicrous for this area; but it is true that you really can't expect public agencies to prepare for a 27-inch storm that demands much heavier equipment than smaller storms, unless you think it's going to happen frequently.'

Here in a nutshell, by the way, is the heart of the dilemma of a modern industrialized country facing adverse weather conditions. Our dependence on the trappings

Abandoned cars on a Buffalo freeway, recognizable only from the 30 mph sign and the line of street-lamps.

of that society—cars, oil and gas from far away—make us *more* vulnerable, not less, than ever before. But how, in the modern world, can governments justify to the tax payers huge investments in machinery 'just in case' the weather turns really nasty? It all depends on just how nasty you expect the weather to be, and that is what this book is all about.

The skiers were out not just in Boston but in other cities, most amazingly in New York, where 13 inches (33 cm) of snow fell on the city in one blizzard on 20 January. Two years ago, it would have been hard to believe that 5th Avenue could be a wilderness, abandoned, even on a week-day, to skiers and the occasional struggling pedestrian. The National Weather Service, having predicted no more than three inches (7.6 cm), admitted 'we did a rotten job this time,' small comfort as the nation's largest city was turned overnight into a ghost town. Several people died of heart attacks shoveling snow; others of carbon monoxide poisoning when, stuck in snowdrifts in their cars, they kept the engines running to provide warmth.

Then came the inevitable aftermath—the flooding as the temperature rose and the snow melted. On 26 January the New York metropolitan area was hit by 2 inches (5 cm) of rain, a temperature rise to 58°F (14°C), 60 mph (96 kph) winds interspersed with fog from the contact of warm air and snowdrifts, then floods as the snow melted. But that was not the end: temperatures plummeted back down to 19°F (−7°C), freezing much of the water into lethal ice sheets across roads pot-holed by the severe weather, riddling even the expressways and closing down many highways. While all this happened in the East, the Midwest was again battered by blizzards.

The cost of the previous winter's storms and the lessons which had been learned for the US were summed up in *Business Week* on 23 October 1978, looking ahead to the winter of 1979. The message then was that 'no one is going to be caught by surprise again,' with some companies revising production methods to reduce dependence on natural gas—crippled during the big freeze of 1978—and many subscribing to private weather forecasting services, or even hiring their own meteorologists.

Researchers at the University of Illinois, quoted by *Business Week*, stuck their necks

A Buffalo resident digs his way out through a mound of snow.

A driver tangles hopelessly with a snow-blasted engine.

Car owners try vainly to help each other through the drifting snow.

out with a forecast that after three hard winters in a row in the US Midwest, the odds should favor a mild winter next. This really was taking their reputations in their hands, for, just as a run of three heads in tossing a coin does not change the odds of 50:50 on getting heads next time, so a run of three hard winters does not mean it is the 'turn' of mild weather next. If anything, such a run indicates a persistent climatic pattern, which might very well run for yet another season (which of course it did).

Among the companies hedging their bets were Westinghouse Electric Corporation, changing its ultraviolet curing process to a new technique using only electricity and requiring just one-third of the energy of the old gas-based process, and the International Harvester Company, which has tried the alternative remedy of providing its own natural gas, drilling no less than 25 wells to take care of business for the immediate future.

But all this is the response of individuals and individual businesses. Did governments and civil servants respond equally rapidly? Not according to Geoffrey Bannister, Dean of the College of Liberal Arts at Boston University (one of the hardest hit regions in 1978). He complained in October 1978 of the failure of the Massachusetts state organization to develop storm emergency plans in the light of recent events, and forecast a return of nightmare conditions if the weather turned as foul again in 1979.

One group that must hope so are the private forecasters, who have seen business increase by 20 to 25 percent in 1978, with

A snow plow rams its way along a snowbound road into Buffalo.

just one company, Accu-Weather Incorporated, in State College, Pennsylvania, forecasting sales exceeding $1 million in the full year for the first time ever. Ill winds blow *some* people good!

America's problems in the 1970s were not unique. Three examples as final reminders that in the mid-1970s, the world as a whole had its weather problems:

On 25 December 1974, while London had just experienced 'the warmest Christmas since 1940,' Darwin, Australia, was struck by a cyclone which 'crushed the city like a matchbox'—the Christmas Day Cyclone, as it is remembered. The death toll was light (by Indian standards, anyway) reaching only a few score. But 25,000 people were made homeless as 90 percent of the buildings in the city were destroyed. One eyewitness told of a car cartwheeling 'head over heels' along a road as the cyclone struck. Deputy Prime Minister Dr Cairns, visiting the scene of devastation, declared that 'the rebuilding of the city will be the greatest national challenge the Australian people have faced in 30 years.'

In September 1976 a more or less 'routine' hurricane—Hurricane Liza—struck Mexico. Liza killed more than a thousand people, ripping its way across La Paz on the Baja California peninsula, making 20,000 or more homeless and destroying a shanty town, Chimitla, on the outskirts of the city when a wall of water from a burst dam swept the fragile shacks away. An expected hazard, perhaps, in western eyes—part of the way of life in that part of the world, and not as newsworthy as the Darwin hurricane (even though the loss of life was ten times greater) but still a grim reminder of the way in which the weather rules the lives of so many.

Droughts in the Sahel region of Africa killed more people in the 1970s than all of the minor wars and guerrilla activity which have captured the limelight in news reports about these impoverished states. Across Gambia, Senegal, Niger, Upper Volta, Cape Verde, Mauritania, Mali and Chad seven million people are perpetually threatened by starvation as the rains have failed year after year. Close to the brink, but marginally less at risk, the populations of Ghana, Guinea, Guinea-Bissau, northern Nigeria, Ethiopia and Somalia ought to have far more to worry about than who is fighting whom, and why.

In the technologically protected countries of the developed world, repercussions from even the most distant blasts of weather force themselves into our awareness. 'Unseasonable' frosts in Brazil in the mid-1970s, for example, were a major contribution to the soaring price of coffee in our supermarkets, price rises which took this once everyday drink into the luxury class, from which it has never fully returned. And when we experience a summer like 1976 in England, or a winter like 1978 in the US, we realize that the whole world is affected by the force of the weather. Only by looking at the global weather machine in total can we hope to understand the run of disasters that hit the world in the 1970s and learn what to expect next.

Two headlines of January 1979 support the idea that the extremes of the 1970s may be the norms of the 1980s.

THE WEATHER
Worst Winter Ever

Unprepared for a deadly change

...ring way to begin the new ...own from the Arctic, ... and gale force ...he

Clockwise from top: Queui...
...early hal...
...st...

WHOLE OF BRITAIN UNDER SNOW

Worst over, but freeze goes on

Niagara, frozen into immobility in early 1978.

NEW YORK'S ICE AGE WINTER

Early 1978 brought to America's east coast the worst conditions for almost a century. In February, a blizzard, raging with the force of a hurricane, dumped between one and four feet of snow, killed at least 56 people, and caused an estimated half-billion dollars' worth of damage. On the coast winds lashed the seas into 50-foot (15-meter) waves. Inland, the Niagara River and Falls turned to ice. Even New York City, which is usually spared the worst rigors of the northeast climate, was paralyzed for 24 hours. Residents were glad it was no worse, for they had barely recovered from a 15-inch (38 cm) fall in the previous month, one that kept commuters at home and reduced the normal mid-week bustle of traffic to a whisper. Of the few pedestrians who ventured outside, some donned skis. Though it was the worst winter anyone could remember, climatologists warned that such cold and snowfalls may become the rule rather than the exception.

A New York street turned to a desert of snow and slush.

Downtown Manhattan, paralyzed and silent after the January downfall.

A few vehicles move through a corridor cleared in the snow.

A skier makes his way easily along 5th Avenue.

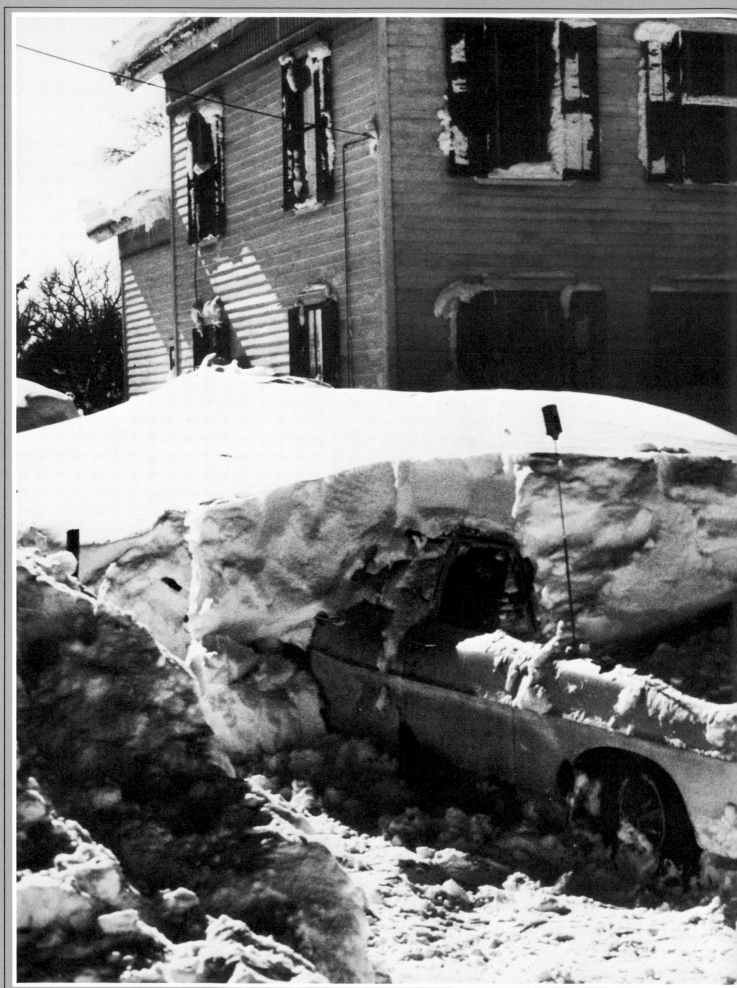

Partially dug out, a car outside a Hamburg, NY, suburban home provides a scale by which to measure the depth of the drifting snow.

New Yorkers dig an exit for their parked car.

After the February storm, locals clear a way through to the sidewalk on W 41st Street.

City engineers clear the Beef Market district of lower Manhattan.

The vast whirlpool structure
of a hurricane, photographed
by Apollo 9 astronauts in
orbit in March 1969, shows
the regularity of form that
lies behind the ferocious and
chaotic effects of such a
storm down on the surface
of the Earth.

2: THE WEATHER MACHINE

Weather is notoriously unpredictable. Locally, its effects often seem random. But there are underlying mechanisms—powered by the heat of the sun—that enable scientists to explain in general terms why the world's climates are as they are.

Our ancestors—and, indeed, many of those from more recent history—regarded the disasters brought by vagaries of the weather as the works of gods. Such phenomena could hit a small agricultural community, could almost wipe it out overnight and literally bring the end of the world as the inhabitants knew it; and how else to explain such a catastrophe except by the act of a god? Today we see local weather phenomena— floods, blizzards, hurricanes, tornadoes—as part of a greater whole, the detailed workings of what author Nigel Calder has called 'the weather machine.' This does not make the disasters any less disastrous, nor does it mean that our now-global civilization is safe from a shift in the workings of the weather machine so great that our entire civilized way of life may be disrupted. But there is comfort to be gained from any understanding of natural forces. Understanding, we

may hope, might one day bring the ability to control these ravaging forces of nature. Let us therefore arm ourselves with a little knowledge about the origin of such forces.

As far as mankind is concerned, weather is a phenomenon of the atmosphere, of air in motion, modified by the way the moving airstreams interact with the land, sea and ice beneath. In simple terms our planet is heated by the Sun's rays unevenly, with much greater heat near the equator (where the Sun stands almost straight overhead at midday) than at the poles, where the Sun's rays strike only glancingly. Convection, the same basic process that stirs the water in a pan heated on a stove, tends to carry the hot air poleward and the cold polar air equatorward in an attempt to balance out the effects of solar heating.

If the Earth were a perfectly smooth,

spherical planet without any spin, that would be the end of the story of weather, with the convection currents becoming perfectly steady winds blowing always in the same direction at the same place on the globe. But the Earth is far from being such a perfect sphere. The effects of oceans and continents produce different kinds of heating in the atmosphere above; winds may be deflected by mountain ranges; and as well as spinning on its axis every 24 hours, giving a sideways twist to the whole pattern of winds, the Earth spins on a slant. In the course of a year, first one pole then the other points towards the Sun, changing the heating pattern again and bringing us the cycles of the seasons.

But there is still some trace of the steady winds of convection that would entirely cover a smooth planet, most especially in the great oceans, away from the polar ice and the land masses, where the trade winds so useful to mariners in the days of sail blow. Without the Earth's spin, hot air from the equator would rise and move straight out towards the poles before cooling, descending and returning at low level to the equator. The 'trade winds' at sea level would blow straight from north and south into the equatorial region. The spin of the Earth, however, puts a twist into the moving airstreams, with the result that in the northern hemisphere these trades blow roughly from the northeast towards the equator, while in the southern hemisphere they blow from the southeast.

Far away from the equator, around the poles, the sea-level winds are dominated by cold air creeping out from the frozen regions, again with a pronounced east-to-west bias in its flow. But in between, at the temperate latitudes of North America and Europe

A warm front moves in from the right over the Midlands of England, towards the town of Stony Stratford. Warm air to the right is rising up over the cold air to the left, forming the cold mass into a wedge shape and condensing to form rain along the front where the two masses of air meet.

(and of part of Australia and New Zealand in the south), the weather is dominated by a strong wind from west to east, high in the atmosphere, which brings at sea level a succession of swirling weather systems, 'lows' or 'depressions,' along the same broad west-east path. This jet stream and its associated low-level weather systems may blow almost directly west to east, carrying a succession of weather systems along the same track; or it may wiggle its way across a broader band of latitudes, travelling first from northwest to southeast, then zigzagging to flow from southwest to northeast before repeating the pattern. This spreads the influence of the weather systems over a much broader belt, with important repercussions on the ground, as we shall see.

This, however, is very much the broad picture. Things like blizzards and hurricanes, intense local rains or regional droughts, are on a much smaller scale. Focusing in on these smaller cogs in the weather machine, we can see the local violence of the weather as a reaction restoring equilibrium after the larger pieces have got 'out of step' in some way—and this occurs all the time, since the atmosphere is never really in equilibrium. In particular, the weather systems of the stormy zone beneath the jet stream are examples of a constant 'fine tuning' of the way the wind blows.

It is at this local level that the weather patterns we all know from television forecasts come into the picture, with the interplay of 'highs,' 'lows' and 'fronts.' Depending on one's point of view, one can regard the fronts and the weather systems behind them either as little eddies on the larger scale flow of high atmospheric winds, or in terms of what happens down below. The 'big picture' is newer, since meteorologists simply did not have good information about the workings of the whole atmosphere of our planet until recently; but the older picture of the relationship between fronts and warm and cold air masses down on the ground is much more relevant in everyday terms to all of us except the specialists studying how atmospheres work. So, recognizing that it is a ground-based view, and an oversimplification at that, I will stick with the older picture here and now.

At its simplest, a 'front' is just the boundary between a mass of warm air and a mass of cold air. Such a front extends at an angle away from sea (or ground) level,

marking the line of a wedge where the warmer air pushes over the top of the colder air. Taking the northern hemisphere as an example, in the stormy zone where such a system begins to develop, the warm air to the south will be moving more or less from west to east, while the cool air to the north, coming out of the polar regions, moves from east to west. The two airstreams then begin to turn about one another, so that a tongue of warm air pushes up into the colder northern air, and a spiralling pattern of winds and fronts— a depression—is formed. The whole system, all the while, drifts from west to east, carrying its spiralling winds with it, under the influence of the broader circulation pattern dominated by the jet stream. On the eastward side of the tongue of warm air in the depression, warm air climbs above the cold air, cools as it does so and deposits its moisture as rain or snow, falling ahead of the arrival of the front at ground level. Behind the tongue, a cold front is produced where cold air pushes under the warm tongue, lifting the warm air up as it does so to produce more rain or snow, this time falling after the front has passed at ground level. Eventually in the spiralling winds the cold front behind will catch up with the warm front ahead, lifting the tongue of warm air completely clear of the ground in an 'occluded front,' where the clouds and rain pass by above with no change in temperature at ground level. The tongue of warm air is pinched out, the 'eddy' in the overall circulation dies away, and the 'low' is filled in by air blowing into the depression from outside until no trace is left.

All the energy to power the winds of such a depression—which may rage as a fierce storm over a local region—comes from the heat liberated as moisture in the form of water vapor which condenses out of the air and falls as snow or rain. In spite of the winds spiralling into its center, often forcibly, a depression is a region of *low* pressure. This is because the air rushing in at ground (sea) level is being pushed up and out at high level from the center of the depression, with the aid of the energy generated by the condensation of water vapor in the weather system.

This may sound complex; but a real weather system is likely to be much more complex still, with perhaps several fronts, and a much more uneven pattern, not

following a simple spiral system of winds. In addition the mobile low pressure systems of depressions have to skirt their way around the more stable regions of high pressure—anticyclones—which are produced where air flows *in* at high level, falls to build up pressure and flows out again, much more gently than the winds of a depression, at ground level. The anticyclones bring settled weather; the depressions can show the power of weather force at its peak.

The most extreme examples of depressions are hurricanes and tornadoes.

Hurricanes are the greatest storms of all—depressions on the grand scale. They build up in the tropics and can sweep across the regions of the temperate zones nearest the tropics—the southern edge in the northern hemisphere and the northern edge in the south. The various regions ravaged by these storms have given them different names: hurricanes in the West Indies and US, cyclones in the Indian Ocean, typhoons in the region of China, Japan and the South Pacific, and willy-willies in Australia. Whatever the name, the storm is of the same type; I shall stick with the term hurricane, the one most familiar in the English-speaking countries of the northern hemisphere.

Hurricanes feed off heat from the warm oceans, where temperatures of the surface waters get above 79°F (26°C), so they can only form near the equator. But they cannot form exactly at the equator, only a little way away where the temperature changes associated with the curvature of the

A hurricane sweeps in over a West Indian island, its winds of over 100 mph (160 kph) whipping waves into a foam and bending palm trees as if they were saplings.

Earth begin to exert their influence on the moving air currents and, with the aid of the rotation of the Earth, wind them up into rotating, spiral systems. Starting out on a course from east to west and away from the equator in either hemisphere, a hurricane will follow a curving path across the cooler waters it encounters, sometimes swinging right around to head almost due east before it dies away. So countries on the western sides of oceans suffer most—China and Japan on the western edge of the Pacific, and the southeastern United States and Mexico on the western edge of the Atlantic. Any hurricane which does curve right around and head back out across the ocean—towards Britain and Europe, in the case of an Atlantic hurricane—will lose strength on the way so that by the time it arrives it will be no more than a fierce depression. The true hurricane must possess winds in excess of 70 mph (112 kph), as well as the whirling spiral winds which make such impressive displays on photographs taken from space.

Hardly surprisingly, it is only very recently that weather men have been able to find out much about what makes a hurricane tick. It takes a brave scientist to make investigations in ships or aircraft subjected to such storms, but studies have been made and are now, of course, aided by satellite pictures. The key feature of such an intense storm is the 'eye' at its center, a region of relatively calm, warm and cloudless air from 9 to 40 miles (15 to 60 km) across, bounded by steep walls of cloud towering to heights as great as 6 miles (10 km) or more above sea level. The eye itself is a region of descending air; the surrounding clouds are produced where air sweeping in from outside at sea level rises and spins around the eye. Such powerful updrafts produce dramatic cooling of the warm air, which is laden with moisture from the sea below, and the result is torrential rain. Farther away from the eye, the swirling mass spreads over a diameter ten times greater, with winds often exceeding 100 mph (160 kph). Once the system is established, drawing energy from the warm ocean below, nothing can stop it until it reaches land, which cuts off the supply of water, or cooler water farther from the equator, which cut off the supply of heat. The whole hurricane system may move at about 30 mph (48 kph), generally giving ample time for it to be tracked and appropriate precautions taken in the region towards which it is headed. But any precautions are likely to prove inadequate in the face of such fierce winds, rainfall of an inch (2.5 cm) or more per hour, and the added risk of flooding from a rise in sea level produced by the very low pressure at the center of the hurricane.

Although hurricanes generally hit only coastal regions, they can on occasion wreak havoc far inland before dying out, as happened in 1938 when a severe hurricane travelled 150 miles (240 km) inland across the New England region of the US, and in 1954 when Hurricane Hazel trailed its devastation from the Caribbean to the Arctic.

Many schemes are afoot to 'tame' such fierce storms, either by finding ways to 'steer' a hurricane out to sea away from land, or by somehow cutting off the growth of a baby hurricane before it can rage out of control across the ocean. But even such seemingly worthwhile endeavors are fraught with dangers, given that all the cogs of the weather machine are interrelated. Hurricanes may cause damage, but a large proportion of the water supply of countries such as Mexico and Japan comes from their rains; cutting off the growth of Atlantic hurricanes might even reduce the rainfall over Europe, away to the northeast. Most worrying of all in the long term to the atmospheric scientists is the possibility that effective hurricane-control would upset the system which shifts warm air from the equator to the poles and thus encourage the spread of polar ice.

Another violent type of storm — the tornado—might bear interference without disturbing the global equilibrium. Tornadoes—or 'twisters'—are small-scale relatives of hurricanes. They are most common in the Mississippi lowland region of the United States, but also occur in other parts of the world and over oceans as waterspouts. No one yet knows precisely how tornadoes form, although they are typically associated with conditions of hot, moist air near the ground surface with a layer of cold air above. A hurricane in miniature, a tornado is only 100 to 200 yards in diameter, a compact whirling wind system in which the air speeds have been estimated at up to 650 mph (1040 kph), but never measured accurately, since any instruments in the path

This idealized diagram of the circulation of the atmosphere shows, at the equator, the spiralling pattern of the trade winds, drawn from east to west by the circulation of the Earth, and turning over upon themselves as the air is progressively heated and cooled. To the north and south of the trades are the Westerlies, and polewards are the polar Easterlies.

The idealized wind patterns shown above are complicated by the uneven distribution of the Earth's land masses and the resulting complexity of the circulation of ocean currents, which at different latitudes may be cold (blue) or warm (red).

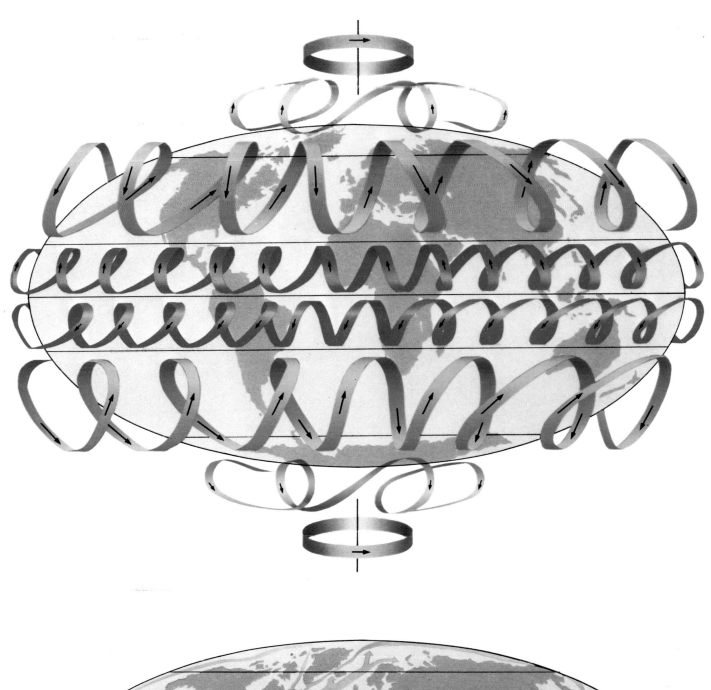

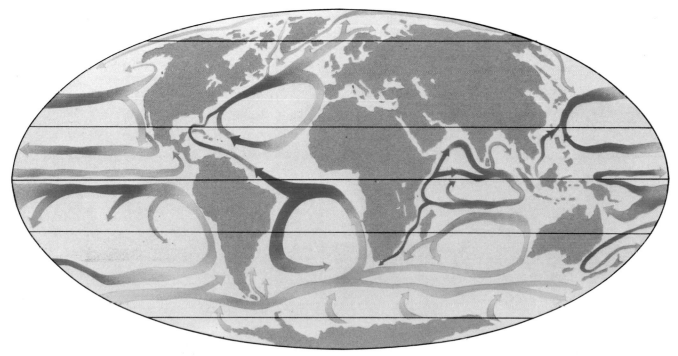

SHOWERS OF FROGS AND OTHER ODDITIES

Among all the serious stories of weather extremes and the disasters they bring, there are many curious and often unexplained anecdotes of bizarre, outrageous or humorous events. These tell us little about the workings of the weather, except to indicate that there is still a great deal we do not understand, but some are surely worth recording in their own right. A great variety of such curiosities can be gleaned from the pages of the *Handbook of Unusual Natural Phenomena* by William Corliss (Sourcebook Project, Glen Arm Maryland, 1977); but many more can be found from perusal of old newspapers on file in any library. What can one make of reports of rain falling from a clear sky? Corliss records six examples of reports of rain or snow from cloudless skies, all of them published in reputable scientific journals. Snowflakes 'larger than milk pans' fell in Montana on 28 January 1887, and a hailstone 6 inches by 8 inches (15 cm by 20 cm) in size, completely enclosing a frozen gopher turtle, fell near Vicksburg on 11 May 1894.

Stories of black snow or colored rain—yellow or red seem to be most common colors can be similarly related to the way the winds sweep dust from dry regions high into the air before dropping it back mixed with water. Here, though, there is genuine information about the workings of the atmosphere to be gleaned, since the kind of dust falling with the rain can often be identified. When Britain is afflicted in this way, it seems that the dust comes from as far away as the Sahara desert in Africa.

Perhaps the oddest phenomenon is 'electric' rain, experienced by an electrical engineer in Cordova, Spain in 1892. After a warm, still day he watched the sky become overcast; at about 8 pm the stillness was broken by one great flash of lightning and peal of thunder, followed by great drops of rain. Each drop, as it reached the ground, gave off a distinct crack and emitted a bright spark of light.

There have been occasional reports of small animals raining from the sky, presumably as the result of whirlwinds sweeping them aloft and depositing them many miles away. Such tales are easily dismissed as fantasy; but they should not be, as the following reports and exchanges taken from the London *Times* of June–July 1939 show:

'Trowbridge (Wiltshire) has been visited by a shower of frogs which apparently fell for a few seconds and within a restricted space.

Mr E Ettles, superintendent of the municipal swimming pool, said that about 4.30 in the afternoon a heavy shower came on and he ran for shelter. As he was running he heard a sound as of the falling of lumps of mud behind him.

"I turned," he said, "and was amazed to see hundreds of tiny frogs falling on to the concrete path surrounding the bath. It was all over in a few seconds, but there must have been thousands of these tiny frogs, each about the size of the top of one's finger. I swept them up and shovelled them into a bucket."

Mr Ettles said he found later that hundreds more had fallen on to the grass on the sunbathing terrace. These he destroyed with a chemical. A few of the frogs had got into the pool, but he was able easily to remove them. Had the main batch fallen into the pool, he said, it would have had to be emptied.

Mr Ettles said he had been twice round the world. "I have seen flying fish and clouds of locusts, but I have never before seen or heard of it raining frogs. It was really an amazing experience."'

'The item in *The Times* of June 17 is interesting to me, as in Madras in November, 1911, as the result of a violent storm which was the prelude to the north-east monsoon, our compound at Adyar House was covered with thousands of tiny frogs. You could step nowhere without treading on them. Mrs G. A. Thomas, 40 Victoria Road, W8.'

'Sir, I noticed a letter in your issue of June 22 headed "Raining Frogs." This reminded me of an experience at Suakim in 1884. When with a company of Royal Engineers we were engaged in making piers, arranging for water supply for means of communication etc preliminary to the arrival of the Expeditionary Force in 1885 which was being organized for the relief of General Gordon, besieged in Khartoum. It was proposed to reconstruct a railway from Suakim to Berber, 25 miles [40 km] of which was actually constructed when the Nile route was adopted in preference to the desert route.

We officers and men were well acquainted with the country up to some 30 miles [48 km] from the coast. The first 10 miles

Edward Cruikshank's 1835 comment on some particularly violent downpours of the time – 'Raining cats, dogs and pitchforks' – serves as an unwitting reminder that clouds can occasionally rain some very strange objects.

[12 km] or so was a waterless scrub-covered desert sloping up to rocky hills and mountains practically bare of vegetation. We never dreamt of the possibility of the existence of frogs: there was no visible water and so far as I can remember, no rain during the year we were encamped in the desert outside the then village of Suakim, except on one day, and then suddenly out of the blue sky appeared a little cloud reminding one of Elijah and the little cloud out of the sea. Then followed torrential rain falling for many hours: it evidently fell on the bare rocky hills inland and the water therefrom rushing down over the 10 miles [12 km] of scrubby desert appeared like a huge lake.

After the storm had subsided and the flood had gone we left our shelters to see what damage had been done to our works. To our utmost astonishment we found the desert land covered with millions of frogs of all sizes. The fierce heat, at one time 125°F [52°C] in the shade, soon killed them and shrivelled them up.
I am. &c. . .
F. C. Heath-Caldwell (Major-General, late RE) Linley Wood.'

'Sir. One of the strangest showers was surely that which fell in Worcester, England, on May 28, 1881. On this day many tons of periwinkles, small crabs, and hermit crabs were found deposited in the streets of Worcester after a violent thunderstorm.

They were quite fresh and the fall was confined to the Cromer Gardens Road area and the fields and gardens contiguous. Mr J Lloyd Bozward, a meteorologist, in an article in the *Worcester Evening Post* for June 9th, 1881, stated that 10 sacks of periwinkles were picked up and sold in the local markets. A man named Maunt collected in his own garden as many winkles as would fill two sacks. As Worcester is many miles from the sea, where did the winkles come from?

Many more instances of showers of living things from the sky could be cited. For example, it "rained frogs" in North London on August 17th, 1921, and showers of little toads fell at Chalons-sur-Saone on September 3 and 4, 1922. There was a shower of snails at Redruth on August 12, 1886, and a vast cloud of red worms descended on Halmstead, Sweden on January 3, 1924. Millions of brown worms dropped from the skies at Clifton, Indiana on February 18th, 1892: and the residents of Frankston, NSW were mystified early in October 1935, by seeing thousands of jellyfish descending from the sky—probably the result of a waterspout somewhere out at sea. . . .
Yours faithfully,
Harry Price. Hon Secretary.
University of London Council for Psychical Investigation, 19 Berkeley Street, W.1. June 29th.'

'With reference to Mr Harry Price's letter . . . it may interest your readers to know that in Bareilly, NWP of India, in 1893, I rode through our barracks and across the parade ground immediately after a heavy storm and cloudburst, and three or four acres of the ground were covered with small fish, about the size of whitebait or small sardine.
Lieutenant-Colonel R C R Owen. Naval and Military Club, 94 Piccadilly, W.1.'

'In May, 1893, when I was in The Royal Sussex Regiment at Dum Dum, torrential rain fell without stopping for a whole week. I happened to be orderly officer for that week and was proceeding towards barracks, during the first downfall, when the surface of the road suddenly became covered with myriads of tiny leaping fishes. I caught huge quantities of these fish by means of a piece of mosquito netting and handed them over to the mess, where they proved excellent.
Lieutenant-Colonel C H Buck, Oakhurst, Yateley.'

of a tornado are inevitably smashed to pieces. Tornadoes travel at about 30 or 40 mph (48 or 64 kph), on straight or twisting, long or short paths, cutting a narrow but severe swathe of destruction across country before blowing themselves out. Although their origins are unclear, the relationship with hurricanes is more than a family one, tornadoes often being born from the disturbance of a hurricane. The classic example is Hurricane Beulah in 1967 which plowed across the south Texas coast and gave rise to a record of 115 associated tornadoes. A few tornadoes are reported even in Britain each year; many more occur over the oceans, to produce waterspouts.

These two diagrams show the major differences between a cold front (left) and a warm front (right). In the cold front, cold air moves in forcing its way underneath warmer air, which condenses as it rises in a billowy cumulus formation. After a certain time, condensation forms drops, which fall as rain. The cloud continues to rise through cold air until, at several thousand feet, it passes a line that marks the freezing point. Here, precipitation is snow or hail, which melts before it reaches the ground. Upper atmosphere winds sweep the top part of the cloud into a characteristic 'thunderhead' shape.

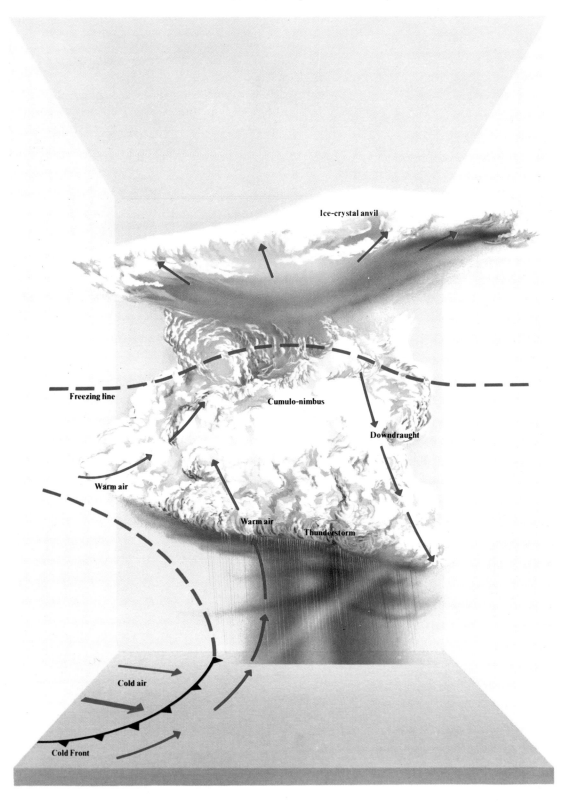

Ice-crystal anvil

Freezing line

Cumulo-nimbus

Downdraught

Warm air

Warm air

Thunderstorm

Cold air

Cold Front

The damaging effect of a tornado is not limited to the strong winds whistling around it, but is also due to the sudden pressure drop at the center. Sucking up water over the sea is relatively harmless, over land this extreme low pressure can cause buildings to explode and can produce weird effects like the rains of frogs, sucked up from marshes and dumped miles away, which have been recorded down the years (see pp. 34–5).

The regions prone to such extremes of weather highlight the way in which life on the Earth's surface depends on the workings of the atmosphere. Where the weather is

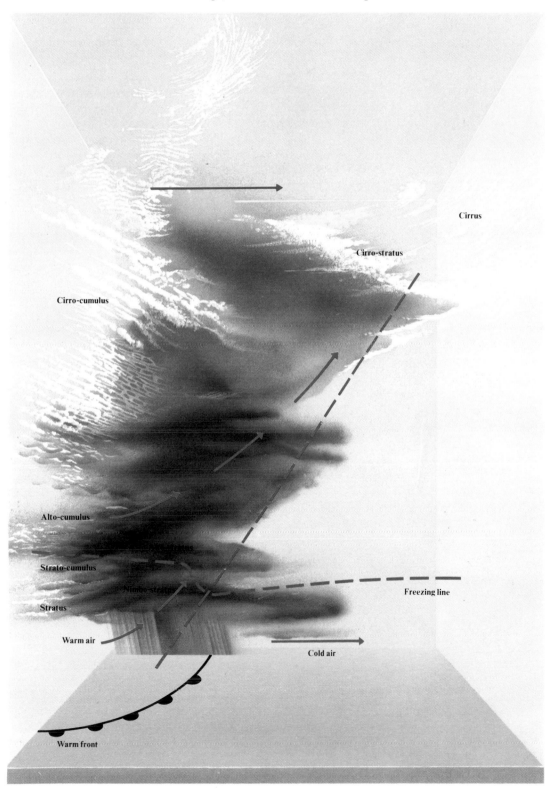

In a warm front warm air moves in from the left and overrides the cold air, condensing at the intersection to form rain.

Cirrus

Cirro-stratus

Cirro-cumulus

Alto-cumulus

Strato-cumulus

Nimbo-stratus

Stratus

Warm air

Cold air

Freezing line

Warm front

extreme, life becomes difficult or impossible; so now, perhaps, it is appropriate to look again at the broader picture, but with special reference to the way the working of the weather machine affects life, including human life, on the surface of the Earth.

The weather zones of the world are roughly distributed in bands of latitude either side of the equator. Because there is more land in the northern hemisphere than in the south, however, the climatic 'equator' does not exactly follow the geographical equator. Indeed this climatic equator—the Intertropical Convergence Zone, or ITCZ— shifts north and south during the year with seasonal changes in atmospheric circulation. The balance of continents and oceans, mountains and plains, also affects the kind of weather occurring 'downwind' in the overall circulation. The overall results give us the climatic zones of the world as it is today.

From about 5° South to 10° North over the oceans and in the steamy river basins of the Amazon and Congo, the islands of Indonesia and the Philippines, Ceylon and the Malay peninsula, the weather is hot and wet—*equatorial* weather, with more or less constant temperatures of around 80°F (27°C) relieved only by the nighttime cooling, which is seldom more than a few degrees. Rainfall in the equatorial zone reaches levels unknown elsewhere in the world, with many sites receiving more than 80 inches (203 cm) a year, and Singapore,

for example, once recording more than 4½ inches (11 cm) in one hour. The heat and wet combine to produce the luxuriant vegetation of the tropical rainforest, but with equal encouragement for disease and insect life this is hardly the best place in the world for human life.

From the equatorial zone to about 20° North or South of the equator the weather is strongly influenced by the trade winds, the returning ground level atmospheric currents from the convective circulation stirred up by the Sun's heat. In the summer in each hemisphere, though, these regions are influenced by the shifting of the ITCZ and its equatorial weather away from the equator, so there is a distinct difference between the dry, trade-wind weather of winter and the wet, sultry summers. These are the *tropical* regions, in weather terms. In dry conditions, with no cloud to block out the Sun, temperatures here can reach above 100°F (38°C), but the same clear skies allow nighttime temperatures to drop below 15°C (60°F). Rainfall averages between 40 and 60 inches (102 and 152 cm) a year, but is strongly affected by the distance from the sea, with the continental interiors much drier and with a stronger difference between the seasons than coastal or island regions. Parts of the tropical weather zone can be very suitable for human habitation, but where the rainfall is unreliable droughts can be common and agriculture difficult. Central America and the northern fringe of Australia are two examples of a well-watered tropical climate with wet summers and almost equatorial vegetation; East Africa, sheltered by the bulge of Africa from damp air from the central Atlantic, is an example of the harsher, drought affected conditions that can also occur within the same broad pattern.

Within the same latitude band, some regions experience a particularly striking effect resulting from the seasonal shift of balance of atmospheric forces. This is the *tropical monsoon* type of weather, which brings a reliable onset of winds off the ocean, carrying rain, at a particular time of year. India is the classic example of a country made habitable for a large population by the rains of the monsoon, although the effect occurs right across southeast Asia— even as far as Japan—and also in West Africa. When the ITCZ shifts north with the onset of northern hemisphere summer,

Saharan dunes, representative of the extreme aridity that borders the tropical regions.

ANATOMY OF A HURRICANE

Hurricanes—which are also known in different parts of the world as tropical cyclones, typhoons and willy-willies—are powered by heat and moisture. They are therefore found near the equator, where the trade winds have space to evaporate sufficient moisture; and they occur only in the 'hurricane season'—in late summer.

First a core of hot, moist air condenses into cumulus clouds which rise. Sweeping in to fill the gap, the prevailing winds create a whirlpool of moist air, building a catherine wheel of clouds that may be several hundred miles across. Towards the center—an area from 10 to 50 miles (15 to 80 km) across—winds may reach 200 mph (320 kph) although in the 'eye' the center from which the clouds spin out, the air is still and clear.

This satellite shot of Hurricane Katrina, sweeping away from Mexico and Baja California in September 1975, shows to perfection the catherine-wheel structure and still 'eye' that typifies the tropical hurricane.

The diagrams on these pages show the principal areas in which hurricanes form and the directions in which they move, as well as a cross-section of the typical hurricane structural plan.

Storms drift westward with the trade wind at about 15 mph (24 kph). They also tend to drift away from the equator until they come under the influence of the Westerlies and reverse their direction. Powered as they are, by hot, moist air, they tend to dissipate their energy when they hit land, unloading their burdens of moisture in dramatic downpours.

Left: A roiling hurricane vortex snapped by Skylab astronauts in February 1974, southeast of New Zealand.

Right: This cross-sectional diagram of a hurricane shows the way in which spinning clouds form into cells. At the base, heavy rain falls. The clouds extend up to several thousand feet above the freezing level (dotted line). In the eye, inside the rapidly spiralling central winds, cold air falls gently.

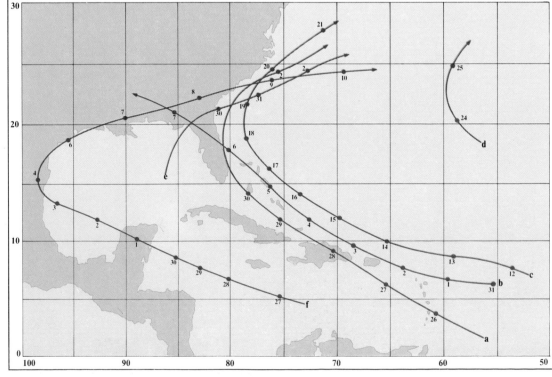

This record of six hurricane tracks was made in 1837 – an early, but typical map of the path, speed and frequency of hurricanes during the 'hurricane season' in the West Indies.

a. Barbados Hurricane
26 July–2 August
b. Antigua Hurricane
31 July–7 August
c. 'Calypso' Hurricane
12–21 August
d. 24–25 August
e. Western Florida Hurricane
30 August–2 September
f. 'Racer's Storm'
27 September–10 October

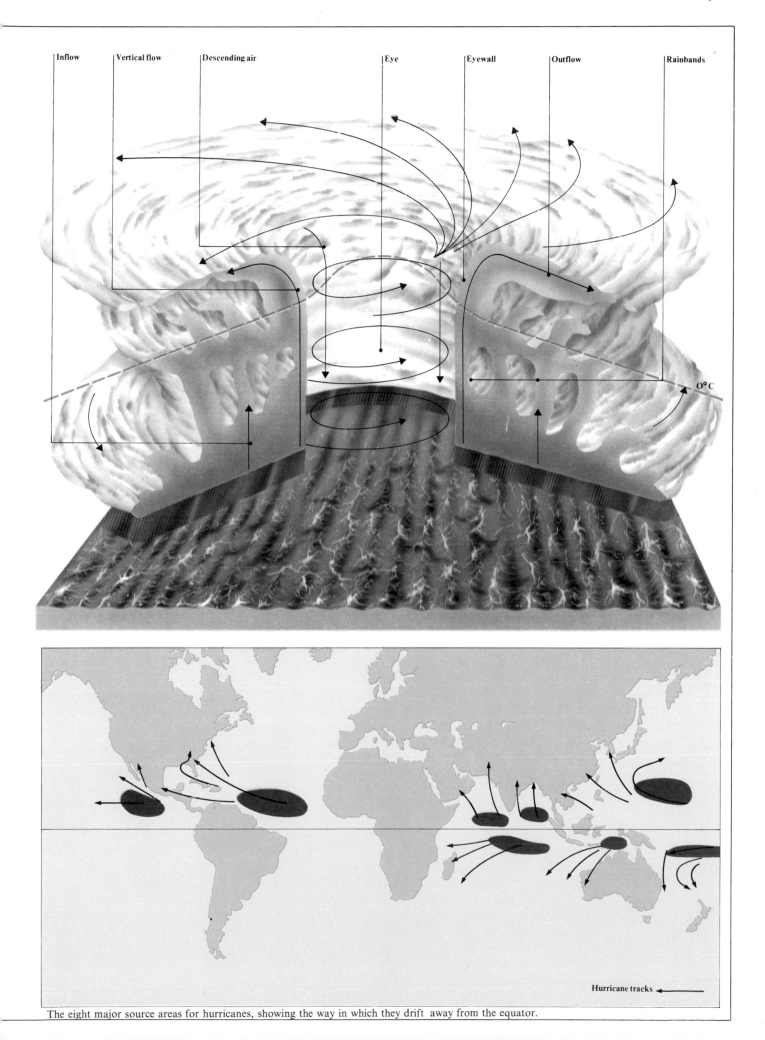

Inflow Vertical flow Descending air Eye Eyewall Outflow Rainbands

0°C

Hurricane tracks

The eight major source areas for hurricanes, showing the way in which they drift away from the equator.

warm, moist air from the ocean-dominated southern hemisphere pushes into these regions, bringing life-giving rain. In India the summer monsoon arrives in the south in late May, and the rains shift northward, reaching the northwest in mid-July. The actual rainfall comes from depressions building up over the ocean and tracking inland—once again, the potential destructiveness of some of these depressions, which may build to hurricane size, has to be balanced against the fact that without them the rainfall to sustain agriculture and the human population would be non-existent. Unfortunately the monsoon rains cannot be completely relied on, especially at their northern limit, and a small shift in the balance of atmospheric circulation is enough to cut off the life-giving rains from the human populations of a belt across Africa and northwest India. Just such a shift occurred in the 1970s, with disastrous consequences that will be discussed later.

Where the monsoon does not penetrate, between about 20° and 30° of latitude, dry weather dominates in the *hot desert* regions of the world. The Sahara and Kalahari deserts, much of central Australia, and the high, dry regions of the western United States are all products of the same dominant weather pattern, almost permanent zones of high pressure and still air between the active winds of the tropical zone and the equally active winds of the temperate latitudes—a kind of still 'buffer zone' between weather dominated by activity from the equator and regions dominated by the circulation around the poles. This is certainly no region for human life, or any other except for a few specially adapted species clinging to the margins where at least some rain falls. Daytime temperatures often climb above 95°F (35°C), with an official record of 136°F (58°C) in Azizia, Libya. Nighttime temperatures in winter plummet to around 40°F (below 5°C) regularly, and frosts are not unknown. The hot deserts are essentially dry. Although enough rain may occur in a year to wet the meteorologist's measuring gauge—no more than 4 inches (10 cm) in an entire year for the Sahara—this rain comes in one or two downpours when wet tropical air penetrates into the desert region erratically and unpredictably. At its borders the desert shades into the surrounding type of climate, perhaps tropical on the equator side, and 'Mediterranean'

at high latitudes.

The *Mediterranean* type of climate gets its name, logically enough, because it is the type of average weather found in the Mediterranean region of southern Europe and northern Africa. Basically this pattern is found on the western sides of continents between about 30° and 40° latitude, so California, southwest Australia and the tip of South Africa all experience a 'Mediterranean' climate. In such regions there is a strong seasonal shift of weather as the atmospheric circulation patterns adjust to changing conditions. Summers are almost like the hot deserts in terms of temperature, dryness, and sunshine; winters produce a penetration of westerly winds bringing moisture from the oceans and plenty of rain. The schoolboy mnemonic for a Mediterranean type of climate remains apposite—'warm, wet westerlies in winter.' This, as anyone who has visited California or Greece will testify, is an entirely acceptable climate for human life. In the hot summer-sun, temperatures may peak above 95°F (35°C), averaging above 75°F (above 25°C) for the warmest month, but the evenings and nights are cool; winters are more like the late spring for a more northern country (such as southern England) and the rainfall, somewhere between 15 and 30 inches (38 and 76 cm), is enough for agriculture while falling in more concentrated bursts than it does at higher latitudes. The rainy days are really wet, but there are many more dry days, and those are really dry.

A little farther away from the equator, however, we come to the region where the weather may be less delightful but is certainly much more interesting: the *temperate* zones, between about 40° and 60° North and between 35° and 55° South, where the westerly winds sweeping around the polar regions dominate. The term 'temperate' is really only appropriate to regions within this zone that lie on the west of continents—such as Western Europe, the northwestern US (excluding Alaska) and New Zealand. (Deep in the hearts of continents—Russian Europe, Siberia or the central-northern US and Canada, for example—there are extreme variations of weather which can hardly be called temperate; these are *continental* climates.) The genuine temperate regions are dominated by the arrival of successive depressions and frontal systems described above. The do-

THE RHYTHM OF THE SEASONS

The cycle of the seasons demonstrates how close we are to a runaway ice age; but why is winter colder than summer, and why does summer come back to melt away those winter snows? This has nothing to do with any change in the *distance* from the Earth to the Sun (although it is true that we are about three million miles [five million km] further away from the Sun during southern hemisphere winter than in southern hemisphere summer). This has a small effect, but is only a tiny fraction in comparison with the average distance of the Earth from the Sun, 93 million miles (150 million km). After all, northern winters are much colder than summer, even though we are then three million miles (five million km) *closer* to the Sun. The true cause of the rhythm of the seasons is the tilt of the spinning Earth, about $23\frac{1}{2}°$ away from the perpendicular to an imaginary line joining the center of the Earth to the center of the Sun, which causes first one hemisphere and then the other to point a little towards the Sun, so that, as seen from the Earth's surface, the Sun climbs higher in the sky of the summer hemisphere.

This not only makes the proportion of daylight hours a greater fraction of the whole 24 hours, reaching the extreme case inside the Arctic and Antarctic circles, the 'lands of the midnight Sun,' but brings the Sun's rays down more nearly vertical at local noon, concentrating their heating effect rather than spreading the warmth over a slanting path. In the winter the opposite happens; daylight hours are reduced (non-existent at the poles), the Sun only rises low above the horizon, and its heat is weakly dissipated over a slanting path across the ground or sea.

The peaks of heat in summer, and the troughs of cold in winter, however, lag behind the apparent position of the Sun viewed from the Earth, because of the time it takes for the Earth to respond to changes in the amount of heat arriving from outside. Taking the northern hemisphere as an example, the Sun rises highest in the sky on 22 June, the longest day, but this is scarcely the beginning of summer proper. As the Sun falls back and the days get shorter into July and August, the heat of summer still builds up to its peak. This is because before June a great deal of incoming heat has gone into warming the hemisphere (rather, the temperate and Arctic zones) after the winter, and even after 22 June for some weeks more heat is coming in from the Sun than the hemisphere is radiating away into space.

In the autumn, this excess heat is only slowly dissipated as the Sun falls lower in the sky and the days shorten, so that the shortest day, 22 December, is far from being the coldest.

Other things being equal, then, southern summers would be a little warmer than those in the north, and southern winters a little cooler than their northern counterparts, in line with the three percent or so change in the distance of the Earth from the Sun. But such a small effect is in any case overwhelmed by the presence of much more extensive oceans in the southern hemisphere than in the north, oceans which warm up less than land in summer, and cool off less in winter, helping to smooth out climatic fluctuations over the seasons. This key role of the oceans also accounts for the relatively small seasonal differences in a maritime country such as Britain, compared with the continental extremes of, say, Canada.

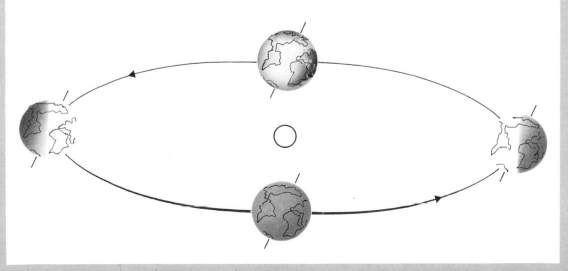

Three contrasting examples of different climatic zones: South American rainforest . . .

. . . the arid wastes of the Western Sahara . . .

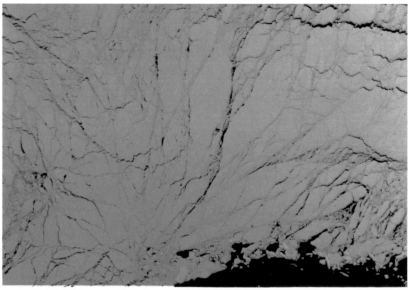

. . . and Antarctic sea ice breaking up during the summer.

minant feature is wet air from the oceans to the west—cooling in summer, warming in winter, and preventing extremes of temperature while bringing plenty of rain. Occasionally very hot air may arrive in summer from the continent, or very cold air may arrive in winter from higher latitudes or the continental interior. By and large, though, this region is wonderful for plant life and quite suitable, though not to everyone's taste, for human life.

In the continental interiors, where the moist westerlies cannot penetrate, life is at once harsher and simpler: hot in summer, cold in winter, and dominated by long spells of uniform weather. This is where the record breaking variations of temperature over the course of a year are recorded—a range of 67°F (37°C) for Winnipeg in Canada—along with severe frosts in the cold, still depths of winter (below 0°F (–18°C) for long spells). One has to be tough to survive at these latitudes in the continental interiors.

Taking the temperate belt as a whole, rainfall, like temperature, covers a wide range of values: more than 100 inches (254 cm) a year on the coasts of Norway or Scotland shading to 20 inches (51 cm) in southeast England and about 20 inches (51 cm) in the interior of continental Europe, with a similar northwest-southeast trend in other parts of the world. Even more significantly, though, the rainfall in the west of the continents is very evenly spread through the year, more than 150 rain days (days with rainfall over 0.008 in or 0.2 mm) in the western coastal margins (and more than 300 rain days in parts of Chile) occurring each year, compared with perhaps 100 a year in the continental depths.

This rather neat pattern is disrupted for North America by the spine of the Rocky Mountains running from north to south just inside the west coast. While the wet westerlies are blocked, the way is opened for cold air to penetrate from the north in winter, and for hot air to sweep up from the south in summer. In spite of these contrasts, however, North America contributes a disproportionate amount of what is the most important product of the temperate zones for a hungry world—the rich grain harvests on which the bulk of the world's population is fed, either directly or after the grain has been 'processed' into meat by being fed to cattle or other animals.

THE CYCLE OF WATER

Perhaps only desert people can truly appreciate the significance of the cycle of water for climate, and thus for life itself. Without the constant turnover of water through evaporation from the oceans and its deposition as rain and snow on land, no higher form of life could have developed on Earth.

Most of the water vapor in the atmosphere —about 84%—comes from the oceans, particularly from equatorial waters. Once in the air, the water vapor is carried about over the globe by wind, condensing back into visible clouds of ice crystals and water droplets, and then falling as rain or snow. Most of the rain falls back directly into the ocean. But the little that falls on land sustains life.

Only a tiny fraction of the Earth's waters are used to maintain this cycle. The total volume of water on the Earth has been estimated at 310 million cubic miles (some 1384 million cubic kilometers), but of this about 97% is always in the oceans. The remaining three percent is at any one time either in the atmosphere or on the land. But most of that three percent—three-quarters of it—is locked in cold storage in the Earth's ice-sheets and glaciers. Almost all of the remainder has soaked into the rock formations that underlie the Earth's soil. The remaining fresh-water is less than one percent of the total; of that, most is in soil, rivers and lakes, and only an infinitessimal 0.035% is at any instant in the atmosphere. Yet so continuous and efficient is the atmospheric machinery that even this is enough to give all land areas an annual rainfall of 35–40 inches (90–100cm) if it were evenly distributed.

Of course it is not evenly distributed. In the wettest of equatorial regions, it rains almost every day; and, in the world's most arid deserts, years may pass between showers. The desert of Turkestan, east of the Caspian Sea, and the Gobi and Takla Makan of Central Asia are deep within continental interiors distant from moisture-laden winds, while the Great Basin of the western United States and the deserts east of the Andes lie in the rain-shadow created by high mountains lying across the path of moist winds.

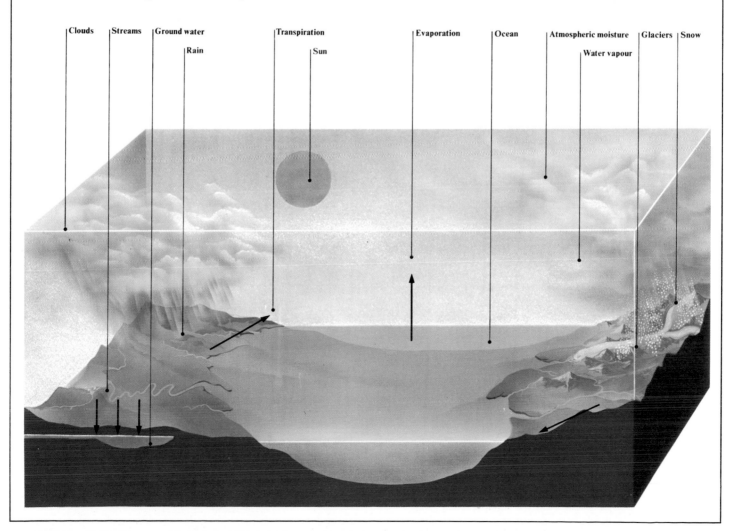

Clouds | Streams | Ground water | Rain | Transpiration | Sun | Evaporation | Ocean | Atmospheric moisture | Water vapour | Glaciers | Snow

RAIN, SNOW, HAIL: PRECIPITATION IN PROFILE

This diagram explains how simple droplets of water vapor come to fall in so many different forms. The seven columns represent the seven categories of precipitation. The horizontal lines divide an idealized cross-section of the atmosphere into the various levels, from the condensation level, which in some clouds may be as high as 23,000 feet (7000 meters), down to ground level.

All forms of precipitation start with water vapor or cloud droplets, several million of which go to make up a raindrop. In freezing clouds, ice crystals form around dust particles of chemical substances. Each droplet or crystal then grows by collision with others, and after 10–20 minutes grows large enough to fall as a raindrop, snowflake or hailstone.

The efficiencies of the natural precipitation processes are low. Although vast amounts of vapor condense into droplets, most of this water re-evaporates. Studies carried out on thunderstorms in the humid eastern part of the US show that only about 20% of the condensed water reaches the ground as rain.

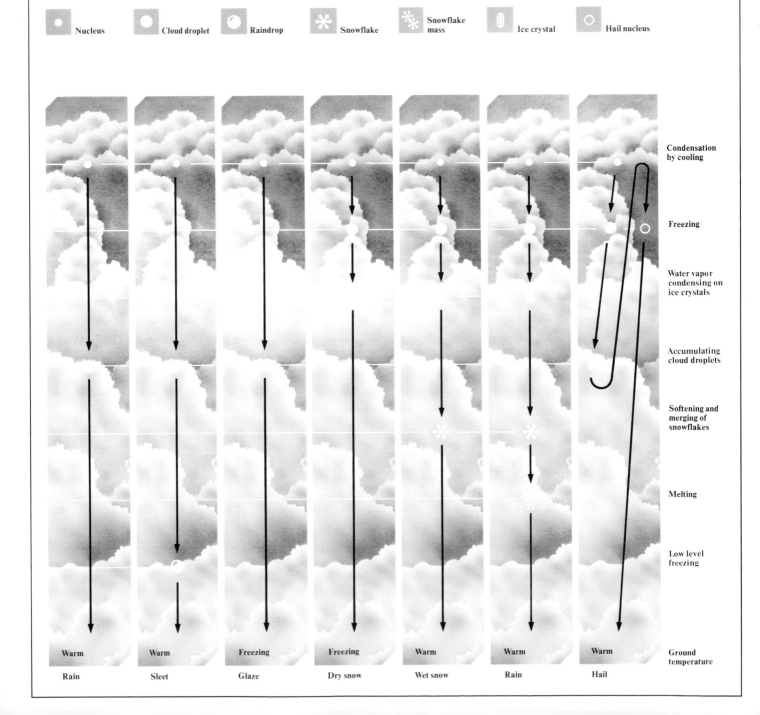

Nucleus   Cloud droplet   Raindrop   Snowflake   Snowflake mass   Ice crystal   Hail nucleus

Rain	Sleet	Glaze	Dry snow	Wet snow	Rain	Hail
Warm	Warm	Freezing	Freezing	Warm	Warm	Warm

Condensation by cooling

Freezing

Water vapor condensing on ice crystals

Accumulating cloud droplets

Softening and merging of snowflakes

Melting

Low level freezing

Ground temperature

At higher latitudes, beyond the temperate zones, lie the regions dominated by *polar* (or *sub-polar*) weather. Temperate lands in both North America and Eurasia are bounded by extensive coniferous forest to the north; in the southern hemisphere the temperate zone is bounded only by cold ocean. Here the winters are long and hard, although summer temperatures can still compare, while the short summer lasts, with those of England, reaching about 70°F (21°C). But the farther north one goes the weaker is the summer influence and the sparser the tree population, shading first into tundra, snow-covered for almost the entire year but with a thin covering of mosses and shrubs in the short summer, and then into the snowy wastelands of the Arctic. In the south this intermediate zone does not exist because there is no land at the appropriate latitudes, and the frozen Antarctic continent is surrounded by sea and pack ice. These are no places for life; the penguins of the Antarctic feed from the sea, not land, and the only human visitors are scientists manning research stations.

The delicate balance which saves us from an equatorward march of the ice after one or two particularly bad winters has been highlighted by studies at the Lamont-Doherty Geological Observatory in New York State, reported by Dr George Kukla in the book *Climatic Change*. As Kukla remarks, 'the South Pole receives more insolation [solar heat] on a summer day than any other place in the world. Yet it is still one of the coldest locations on Earth.' The reason for this is that snow and ice reflect away from their shiny white surfaces almost all of the heat that arrives from the Sun.

If snow and ice cover could once extend far enough down into the temperate zone, it would reflect so much insolation that all the Sun of summer would be insufficient to melt it again, and a new Ice Age would be upon us. Whereas bare grass or forest reflects only 15 percent of incoming heat from the Sun, fresh snow covering the same surface raises the reflecting power (*albedo*) above 80 percent. How much extra snow and ice cover would be needed to tip us inexorably into a new Ice Age?

In one remarkable year recently the cover, monitored by satellites orbiting above the Earth, increased from below 13 million square miles (33 million square km) in the northern hemisphere to nearly 15 million square miles (38 million square km) in 1971–72. This was much greater than the 'normal' year to year variation, and Kukla estimates the increase of two million square miles (five million square km) of snow and ice cover as about one sixth of the total needed to start a new ice age. Six winters like that is all that stands between a pleasant life in the temperate zone and the eternal snows now restricted to higher latitudes. Fortunately, following 1974 there was a fairly steady decline in snowcover back down towards the pre-1971 levels. But two more very severe northern winters, in 1977 and 1978, have served as another reminder of just how literally the seasonal variations at high latitudes mimic the arrival and retreat of the Ice Ages. Human life in the temperate zone really is balanced on the see-saw of the seasons—and it is quite possible for that see-saw to swing much further into cold than we have been used to for a century or more.

All of this pattern shifts with the seasons—a regular pulse of change which plunges first one hemisphere then the other into the beginnings of an Ice Age each year before relenting. Suppose one year the pattern got 'stuck' in some way and winter never left—a prospect which some scientists now hold up as the probable way in which a new Ice Age begins, once all other conditions are right.

If that happened the temperate zone would become uninhabitable, at least for the large populations which now live there; the Mediterranean climates would be much less pleasant; the deserts as bad as ever; and only in the tropical region and the equatorial zone could life continue as 'normal,' apart from the disruption caused by the ripples from the disaster at higher latitudes. This is the knife edge on which human society balances, with the uncomfortable knowledge that Ice Ages have been much more common than the conditions we now enjoy for at least the past few hundred thousand years of the Earth's long history. More of this follows in Chapters 4 and 5; but first look at how the restless stirrings of the weather machine, even while bringing life-giving rains and summer warmth to much of the world, inevitably also bring killing winds, freezing storms and other disasters.

Six examples of the apparently infinite variety of snow crystals.

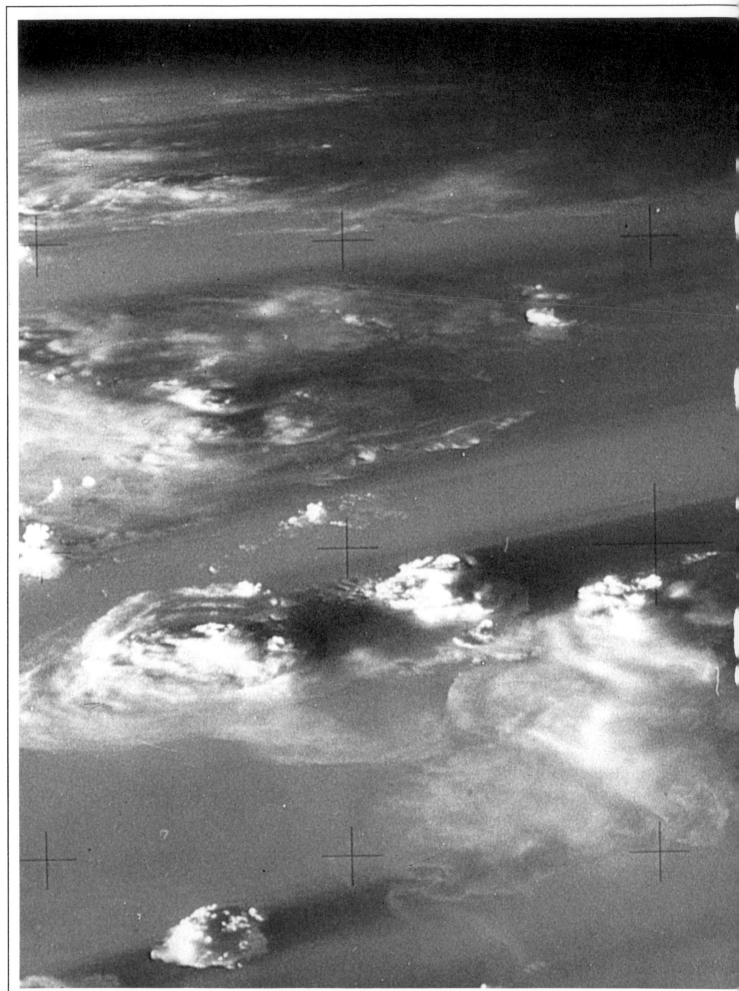

This Skylab shot shows cumulonimbus thunderheads bubbling up through a colder surrounding cloud blanket.

CLOUDS IN FORMATIO

Although the best known clouds are probably the billowy, fluffy cumulus forms—seen from above in the two unusual satellite shots on this page—there are, in fact, ten main families of clouds, which are further subdivided into 14 'species' by meterologists. A selection is shown on the following pages.

The normal classification describes clouds according to the height at which they are usually found:

High—16,500 to 45,000 feet (5000 to 14,000 m): Cirrus, Cirrocumulus, Cirrostratus.

Middle—6500 to 23,000 feet (2000 to 7000 m): Altocumulus, Altostratus, Nimbostratus.

Low—to 6500 feet (2000 m): Stratocumulus, Stratus, Cumulus, Cumulonimbus.

The shapes are also linked by a cause-and-effect relationship. Filmy stratus clouds, formed where hot and cold air meet, range from low-lying fog (although fog is itself of several types, with their own causes)—to whispy cirrostratus. The four forms of cumulus are caused by convection, an updraft created when hot air, rising through cold air, cools and condenses.

Finally, there are wave clouds, which give little indication of weather conditions because they are formed—occasionally into extraordinary shapes—by wind deflected to a different temperature level by mountains.

Thunder-clouds boiling up over the Amazonian jungle.

Warm and cold air meeting along the English coast at Ramsgate, Kent, create a miniature range of low-lying stratus.

Fog, caused by warm, moist air blowing in over cold water, blankets the Forth Bridge.

Individual clouds of fairweather cumulus.

A towering cumulonimbus.

Cumulus clouds, caused by the upward convection of warm air, can take many forms. They may be the low-lying fair-weather fluff-balls familiar on hot summer days; or the soft, woolly blankets, often seen from airplane windows; or the towering heaps and pillars that signal the formation of a thunderstorm. These often have their tops swept flat to create anvil shapes—or 'thunderheads' —by upper-atmosphere winds. Thunderheads often rear up above surrounding cloud-forms.

Cumulus clouds are most common over land by day in summer, when the warm ground creates updrafts, and over the oceans in winter, when cold air blows in from north and south over the warm water towards the equator.

The high-lying, streaky cirrus clouds are usually associated with ice-particles forming in the upper atmosphere. Sometimes the icy filaments form rippling cirrocumulus, or which produce ghostly halos round the Sun and Moon.

Low-lying stratocumulus.

A blanket of altocumulus.

Altocumulus at sunset.

Streaky, high-lying cirrus over Great Salt Lake, Utah, at sunset.

An extraordinary wave-form cloud over a valley in New Zealand.

A UFO-like wave-form over Mount Rainer, Washington.

3: A ROLL CALL OF DISASTERS

Although some areas are more at risk than others, we all live under the threat of climatic disaster of one kind or another. Floods, droughts, hurricane-force winds — all provide reminders of our dependence on the vagaries of our weather system.

This is reputedly the
most remarkable tornado
photograph ever taken.
The twister swept through
Jasper, Minnesota. Tornados
provide the most dramatic
illustration of the immense
forces that can be focused
and unleashed by our
atmosphere.

In any roll call of weather disasters one must have pride of place—Noah's Flood, which in Biblical legend inundated the whole world (that is, the world of the Mesopotamians). Although the story that has come down to us seems to have grown somewhat in the telling, there seems very little doubt that the events described in the Bible (and another great epic, *Gilgamesh*) are founded on a number of actual floods which inundated much of the Tigris-Euphrates valley in the fourth millennium BC. Stories of the great floods were handed down by word of mouth for generations until eventually—well over a thousand years later—they were fixed in writing.

Noah's Flood is of considerable interest to historians and archeologists, but it is impossible as yet to say why it—or they—occurred. One hypothesis is that the flooding may have been related to the melting of the great ice sheets at the end of the most recent Ice Age. But the glaciers had retreated to their present positions by 8000 BC; there is a 4000-year gap between the ice's retreat and the Mesopotamian floods.

Today we are hardly likely to suffer the problems that faced Noah. It is more likely that we are in an inter-glacial period and we will have to face the problems of the *beginning* of an Ice Age, not the results of further melting. In tribute to Noah, though, let us start our rundown of weather disasters by looking at floods—and noticing, incidentally, how very little is recorded about *any* floods that occurred more than a hundred years or so ago.

We can, however, go back just over 200 years to find a detailed record of a flood which in November 1771 devastated northern England. It inspired a later resident of North Yorkshire, Thomas Jackson Foggitt, to devote a lifetime to the study of the weather and, in particular, to gather details of the disaster. The flood swept away half of the North Yorkshire town of Yarm, an event remembered so vividly that his boyhood (Foggit was born in 1809) was colored by tales of the disaster from his grandparents and aged neighbors.

Foggitt quoted a letter from Barnard Castle in County Durham dated 19 November 1771:

'I am sorry to aquaint you with a dreadful calamity that has befallen this place from an inundation. By an incessant rain which fell from Friday morning to Saturday night, the River Tees swelled to such a degree, as to rise upwards of 20 feet [6 m] perpendicular, higher than the oldest man living can remember. The first appearance of its rise was perceived about 4 on Saturday afternoon, and in the space of 4 or 5 hours, the butt end of the bridge, on the south side of the river, was swept away. Mr Newton, Mr Birbeck, Mr Chapman, Mr Sparrow, Mr Scott, Mr W. Monkhouse, Mr Coates, Mr Baxter, Mr Wrightson, and several more, had their dwelling houses, workhouses, with all their stock in trade, furniture and wearing apparel, likewise swept away; nothing in short was safe but the clothes they had on. On the north side of the river, from below the bridge down to

A 19th-century drawing combines meteorological phenomena.
1 & 2. Effects of wind on land and sea.
3. Waterspouts.
4. Fog.
5. Stratus clouds.
6. Cumulus clouds.
7. Cirrus clouds.
8. Nimbus clouds.
9. Cirrocumulus clouds.
10. Rain.

11. Snow.
12. Perpetual snow.
13. Glaciers.
14. Aurora Borealis.
15. Rainbow.
16. Halo.
17. Mirage.
18. Mock Suns.
19. Zodiacal light.
20. Will o' the wisp.
21. Lightning.
22. Lightning conductor.
23 and 24. Shooting stars.

Horngate Wynd, about ¼ mile [400 m] in length, all the workhouses, dry houses, tan yards, and everything adjoining to the river, are entirely gone. About ¼ mile [400 m] below the town, a corn mill with outhouses and stabling belonging to the Rt Hon Lord Darlington was taken down by the impetuosity of the current. At Greta Bridge, several houses, along with the bridge, are taken away, likewise the bridge between Norton and Rokeby Hall. We have dismal accounts of what has happened below us. At Yarm, one half of the town is entirely swept away, and unfortunately 46 persons missing. We have received divers accounts of the same accidents happening in Northumberland, Cumberland and Westmorland. In short, this place discerns a scene of

horror and desolation too dreadful for humanity to behold or words to express.'

Of course every flood is the 'worst ever' to those who experience it. But the events of 1771 really do stand out even in an objective study. Of 14 bridges on the Tyne only one was left standing, and that was damaged; at Bywell Village, almost every house was swept away and graves washed open so that the living, the dead and the long dead were washed along together in a grisly flotsam; 34 ships were wrecked on the bar off Sunderland.

At the same time, across the narrow neck of England on the west coast at the Scottish border near the Solway Firth, the heavy rains had a peculiarly bizarre consequence, when the mossy top of a low hill, the 'Solway Moss,' literally came apart and swamped whole villages in peaty mud. Again Foggitt recorded the story as told to him: 'The interior part of the hill seems to have been nothing but a vast collection of mud, so much diluted with the waters of the springs, dispersed in several parts of it, as to have a considerable degree of fluidity. It had always been, even in the driest summers, so much of a quagmire, that it was hardly safe for anything heavier than a sportsman and his gun . . . .

'Hitherto the shell of more solid earth, in which this fluid moss was enclosed had been sufficient to resist the pressure; but its force, with its fluidity, having been considerably augmented by the late excessive rains, it forced a passage at the eastern extremity . . . . Having once made a breach it soon enlarged it, and poured a deluge of mud into the valley, which runs along the bottom of the hill . . . .

'Of the villages one or two have entirely disappeared; of others the thatch is only visible, and all of them to the number of 13 or 14 are entirely uninhabitable. The greater part of the plain on which they stood was laid out in fine enclosures; the hedges of which, though 8 or 9 feet (2.4 or 2.7 m) high, are now totally invisible . . . .

'In the meantime, the Moss itself, which was before a level plain, on the top of a hill, is now a valley . . . .'

Coming forward to our own century, we have much more than anecdotal material as a catalog of disaster. Photographs, films, scientific measurements and all the paraphernalia of the 20th century combine so that some of the time the flood seems

60/

Two contemporary prints record (top) 'certain wonderful flowings of waters' in 1607 and (bottom) the floods and storms of 1613.

to be a paper one of reports and statistics. How does one interpret in human terms such statistics as '140,000 made homeless' as in the Ohio–Mississippi floods of January 1937? But often some smaller item may catch the eye to individualize the event. In this case Franklin D Roosevelt was re-

ported taking the oath of office at the start of his second term in the cold and intense rain which kept so many people indoors that the President, icy wind beating into his face, addressed 'one of the smallest immediate audiences in the history of inaugurals.' This is the kind of occurrence that puts a human face on the statistics of events. At the same time, in Pittsburgh, Pennsylvania, the National Guard was mobilized as rivers rose 33 feet (10 m) above normal; 70 feet (21 m) of flood-water slammed through Cincinnati, causing damage estimated at $5,000,000 (in 1937 prices!). Small wonder that the President took personal control over organizing the response to the disaster.

World-wide, such floods are common events, especially in autumn. One student of weather analyzed the reports of severe weather conditions appearing in English newspapers over the four months September to December 1976. There were no less than 22 floods, world-wide, which had been damaging enough to gain attention in the media. That is a rate of two severe floods almost every week—and takes no account of the presumably larger numbers of floods that are personal disasters for many people but not 'newsworthy.' Just one such disaster must stand for the many—a flood which affected millions of people in one of the poorest parts of the world, a typical example in its way, mainly because it was linked with a hurricane.

The hurricane that on 12 November 1970, hit East Pakistan (now Bangladesh) was uncommon only in its power. The torrential rain combined with a tidal wave to sweep across 10,000 square miles (26,667 sq km), leaving refugees huddled on hilltops above the waters, while the limited relief services available attempted to get food and other aid to them by helicopter. The correspondent of the *Pakistan Observer* reported the scene that met him at one village:

'Bodies which could not be buried have started decomposing. The air is filled with a bad smell, and the small number of survivors are without food. I saw about 800 bodies lying on both sides of the dam badly damaged by the tidal wave. I found one or two survivors in each house, mostly women and children.'

Another reporter in the Ganges delta area wrote: 'I saw at least 3000 bodies littered along the road. Survivors wandered

Three shots taken shortly after torrential rain and a tidal wave swamped thousands of square miles in Bangladesh, 1970.

A woman's corpse emerging from the flood-waters.

A victim in a ruined house.

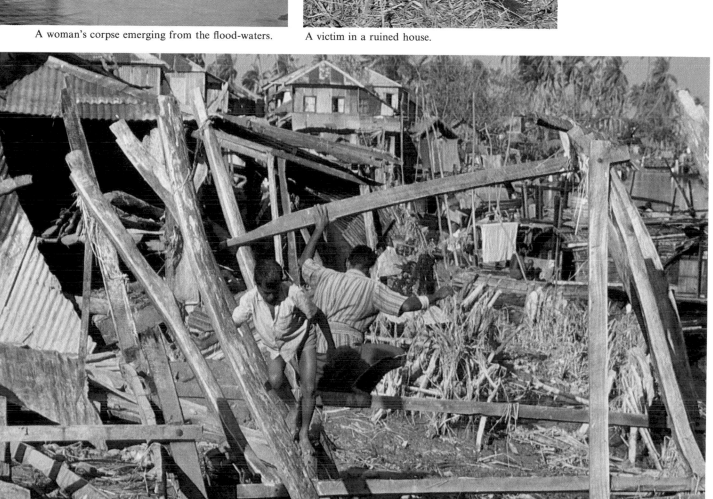

A flooded village.

like mad people, crying out the names of their dead ones. There were 5000 bodies in graves, 100 to 150 in each grave.'

No one knows how many were killed. The government, trying to play down the scope of the disaster, put the total at a few score thousand—'only' a few score thousand. Unofficial estimates set the figure ten times higher—perhaps half a million people killed in one flood disaster. A week after the disaster, as helpers struggled into the devastated region, they found that in some areas they could not walk without treading on the bodies of the dead which carpeted the villages, and that many bodies were left hanging in the trees by the receding flood-waters. Two and a half million people were made destitute by the flood; deaths from starvation and disease added to the toll over the weeks of November and into December and the new year of 1971, with the official death figures then rising to 150,000, and unofficial estimates climbing in proportion to two million. The enormous scope of the disaster, the bitterness felt by survivors who, rightly or wrongly, blamed the government based in West Pakistan for the inadequacy of aid and rebuilding in its wake, played no small part in the events soon after, when, after a harsh struggle, East Pakistan achieved independence as Bangladesh. It was perhaps the poorest nation on Earth, born out of one disaster and heir to many more to come.

By any of its many names, the hurricane or cyclone is the most violent weather system encountered on Earth. It brings not only flooding, but winds of terrifying force. The main (though not the only) hurricane zones of the world are still (a) the West Indies and the southwestern US, where hurricanes boil up in the tropics to track westward before they curve away northeast and fade away, and (b) the regions of India and Bangladesh. The origins of hurricanes have already been described in Chapter 2; their effects can be as devastating as a nuclear war.

Few detailed accounts survive of major hurricanes before about 1900. Yet one storm —that of 1703—was so extraordinary that it can be recalled today as vividly as a recent disaster. For one thing, it occurred in Britain; for another, it was unprecedented in violence. Even as the tail end of a hurricane, and even after crossing the Atlantic into Europe, it has gone down in English

A flood sweeps Yuba City, California, December 1955.

A cow suspended after a flood on the Cumberland River, Kentucky, in 1973.

THE POWER OF FLOODING WATERS

With the exception of the Great Basin of Nevada and the arid southwest, no region of the US is immune from floods in any month of the year. But the area east of the Mississippi, where dry, cold air masses meet warm, moist air originating in the Caribbean and south Atlantic, is particularly subject to storms and floods. The Mississippi inundated vast areas seven times between 1884 and 1952. In July 1942 in Pennsylvania, 30 inches (76 cm) of rain fell in 12 hours.

In 1936 all the New England states were flooded. In March when heavy rain began to melt the snows of winter, the waterways rapidly became choked with thawing ice and rainwater. Dams gave way and bridges were swept away. When more rain moved in from the south, many areas received four inches (10 cm) during a two-day downpour. This, combined with the remaining snow, amounted to 10–30 inches (25–76 cm) of water spread over the whole New England area.

In August 1955 southern New England received another soaking from two hurricanes, Connie and Diane. At Westfield, Massachusetts, close to the Connecticut border, an incredible 18 inches (46 cm) of rain fell on 19 August—an all-time record for New England. At Hartford, Connecticut, where the height of the Connecticut River has been monitored for 300 years, the waters rose to 30 feet for the third time ever. In Putnam, the river leapt its banks and swept down the High Street. Eighty-two died, 5000 were injured, and damage exceeded $800 million.

The river in Putnam, Connecticut surges over its banks and down the city's main streets in August 1955.

Tissues soak the moisture from a 16th-century Madonna by Cranach.

THE GREAT FLORENCE FLOOD

Florence has never been sacked, but it has on several occasions been devastated by floods, the most disastrous of which occurred in November 1966. The Arno rose six yards and deposited mud, debris and oil through thousands of buildings. Notable casualties were the Archaeological Museum's Etruscan collections and Cimabue's 'Crucifix' in the Museo di Santa Croce. Several libraries and archives were completely flooded in mud and water. Fortunately an army of volunteer workers arrived from all over the US and Europe to save the damaged paintings and books.

Below: Troops rescue some of the 100,000 made homeless by the flood.

Bottom: Inside the Basilica of Santa Croce, a soldier shovels up mud.

history as the Great Storm. It struck on 26 and 27 November 1703 and caused more damage, with a greater impact on the minds of the people of the time, than any other storm in the history of the British Isles. Given the reputation of British weather, that is an awesome comment on its power.

We are particularly lucky in having an account of the impact of this storm from one of the masters of storytelling, Daniel Defoe—but his account is reliably recorded as unembellished, with no element of fiction. The 26 November (6 December in the new calendar which was adopted in 1752 and which we use now) was a Friday; during the day atmospheric pressure fell and winds from the south-southwest built up to gale force, reaching a peak of violence in the West Country around midnight. The great Eddystone lighthouse was washed away without trace (along with its designer who had the misfortune to be visiting it at the time); winds piled water into the Severn estuary and river valley, flooding the town of Bristol and surrounding countryside and drowning thousands of sheep and cattle, toppling church steeples and ripping lead roofs.

The barometer was available in the early 18th century, if only in limited numbers, and the measurements that were made indicate that the center of this Great Storm—a true hurricane, even when it hit Britain passed near Liverpool. Travelling eastward, the central fury of the storm reached London at about 3 am on the Saturday morning, sending chimneys and roof tiles crashing into the streets and making it impossible to venture out of doors until about 8 am, when battered Londoners emerged to find their city a shambles and 700 ships in the Thames blown together into a great watery traffic jam in a river bend. Again the effects can only be likened to those of war—in particular, to the massive bombing raids which London experienced in the 1940s.

But at least London houses were chiefly built of brick, and they gained some protection from each other. In the countryside, where many houses were still made of wood and stood in isolation, the impact on individuals and families was even greater. Hundreds of houses were completely destroyed, along with thousands of uprooted trees; on the Isle of Wight, salt spray blown inland covered the grass, which cattle refused to eat, and similar crustings of salt were noted in Sussex and Kent on hedges and trees a full 25 miles (40 km) from the sea. On land the loss was chiefly material—£100,000 pounds worth in Bristol alone, where imported goods from America and the West Indies were flooded in store, destroying 1000 hogsheads of sugar and 1500 of tobacco. At sea the loss of life was terrible. Protected by their buildings, land-lubbers suffered, but only a few hundred at most were killed. Seamen had no protection as their ships foundered under them, with accurate naval records showing 1500 dead and best estimates of the total loss of life being around 8000.

Could such a storm come again to Britain? The answer must be yes since the basic pattern of the weather is much the same now as in the 18th century. If anything, as later chapters of this book will show, weather conditions now are becoming more like 18th century weather than any decades so far in the 20th century. A grim, if un-likely, prospect remains that where such a storm has struck once a similar one could strike again.

One of the greatest hurricanes of historical times, the Great Hurricane of 1780, caused far more havoc than any contemporary war, completely destroying an English fleet off St Lucia in the West Indies, sinking 40 ships in a French convoy near Martinique and ravaging the island itself, bringing death to 9000 people. Along the chain of

THE GREAT STORM

'The Great Storm' (as it is always known) that struck England in November 1703 entirely justifies its title. It destroyed more property and caused the death of more people, both on land and sea, than any other known English storm. It was the only known tempest which at that latitude has equalled the rage of a tropical hurricane. No other tempest—as the great historian Macaulay recorded—was ever the occasion of a parliamentary address or of a public fast. Whole fleets were wrecked. London and Bristol were left like cities sacked.

From the few barometric observations of the storm which have been preserved it seems that the storm's center passed roughly over Liverpool, and moved across England in an easterly direction. Its greatest fury was experienced south of a line from the Bristol Channel to the Thames. The effects of the gale, which began on the afternoon of the 26th, were recorded by the novelist Daniel Defoe. Tiles, coping stones, and chimney pots fell in such profusion that it was dangerous to be out of doors. Yet the houses were so rocked by the wind that many were afraid to stay indoors.

Church-roof lead was rolled up 'like cloth' and carried away. In Kent whole orchards were flattened. According to Defoe's estim-ations—based on letters from all over the country—tens of thousands of trees were uprooted, and 14,000 houses destroyed. Some 8000 died.

One of the most remarkable of the letters, from the parson of Besselsleigh near Oxford, describes one of the few fully-fledged tor-nadoes in British records. The tornado, which swept across Oxfordshire, preceded the full impact of the storm. The description is of interest not least because the country parson's ignorance led him to invent an emotive turn of words to describe the phenomenon and to regard it without the fear that normally seizes observers in, say, the American Midwest.

'On Friday, the 26th November, in the afternoon, about four of the clock, a country fellow came running to me in a great fright, and very earnestly entreated me to go and see a pillar, as he called it, in the air in a field hard by. I went with the fellow: and when I came, found it to be a spout marching directly with the wind. And I can think of nothing I can compare it to better than the trunk of an elephant, which it resembled, only much bigger. It was extended to a great length, and swept the ground as it went, leaving a mark behind. It crossed a field, and what was very strange . . . meeting with an oak that stood towards the middle of the field, snapped the body of it asunder. Afterwards, crossing a road, it sucked up the water that was in the cart-ruts. Then, coming to an old barn, it tumbled down . . . After this I followed it no further . . . But a parishioner of mine going from hence to Hinksey, in a field about a quarter of a mile off of this place, was on the sudden knocked down, and lay upon the place till some people came by and brought him home.'

islands north to Puerto Rico the devastation carved its swathe, and as the hurricane weakened and bent away northeast past the Bermudas and back into the Atlantic it was still powerful enough to sink several English warships en route to Europe.

In 1886 Texas was struck by a veritable plague of hurricanes. One storm passing near Sabine, Texas, in June caused extensive flooding; in August an even more severe hurricane swung in from the Caribbean, passing San Antonio at 2.40 pm on the 20th having virtually destroyed Indianola on the way; in September a lesser storm swept over the coast near Brownsville for a brief visit; and in October yet another hurricane chose Sabine as its target, causing flooding 20 miles (32 km) inland which shifted every house in the area on its foundations and killed 150 people.

But these four hurricanes together had far less impact than the disaster of September 1900 when Galveston was wrecked by a hurricane. Reaching the Texas coast on 8 September 1900, this was a storm of spectacular fury, bringing with it a surge of sea water to flood the city at the mouth of Galveston Bay. More than six thousand people were killed; property damage climbed above $20,000,000. The New Orleans *Daily Picayune* carried first reports of the full extent of the disaster on Monday 10 September: 'The hurricane . . . was the worst

THE 1780 HURRICANE

In October 1780, a hurricane—still referred to as 'The Great Hurricane'—hit Barbados, raged on to St Vincent and Martinique, crossed the eastern Caribbean, and wheeled north to Bermuda, where it drove 50 vessels ashore. It finally died away in mid-Atlantic, having killed some 20,000 people. There has been preserved a first-hand account of this hurricane's violent passage over the island of Barbados, written by the island's Governor, Major General Cuninghame:

'The evening preceding the hurricane, the 9th of October, was remarkably calm, but the sky surprisingly red and fiery; during the night much rain fell. On the morning of the 10th, much rain and wind from the NW. By ten o'clock it increased very much; by one the ships in the bay drove; by four o'clock the *Albermarle* frigate (the only man of war then there) parted her anchors and went to sea, as did all the other vessels, about 25 in number. Soon after, by six o'clock, the wind had torn up and blown down many trees and foreboded a most violent tempest. 'At the Government House every precaution was taken to guard against what might happen; the doors and windows were barricaded up, but it availed little. By ten o'clock the wind forced itself a passage through the house from the NNW and the tempest increasing every minute, the family took to the center of the building, imagining from the prodigious strength of the walls, they being three feet thick, and from its circular form, it would have withstood the wind's utmost rage: however, by half after eleven o'clock, they were obliged to retreat to the cellar, the wind having forced its way into every part, and torn off most of the roof. . . .

'Anxiously did they wait the break of day, flattering themselves that with the light they would see a cessation of the storm; yet when it appeared, little was the tempest abated, and the day served but to exhibit the most melancholy prospect imaginable; nothing can compare with the terrible devastation that presented itself on all sides; not a building standing; the trees, if not torn up by their roots, deprived of their leaves and branches; and the most luxuriant spring changed in this one night to the dreariest winter. In vain was it to look round for shelter; houses, that from their situation it was to have been imagined would have been in a degree protected, were all flat with the earth, and the miserable owners, if they were so fortunate as to escape with their lives, were left without a covering for themselves and family. . . .

'Nothing has ever happened that has caused such universal desolation. No one house in the island is exempt from damage. Very few buildings are left standing on the estates. The fortifications have suffered very considerably. The buildings were all demolished; for so violent was the storm here, when assisted by the sea, that a twelve-pound cannon was carried from the south to the north battery, a distance of 140 yards [128 m].'

The ports of India have few defenses against typhoon winds and floods. At right is a classic shot of Bombay harbor after being struck by a typhoon in 1856.

A typhoon hits Calcutta in the mid-19th century.

Flood waters in Calcutta in the 1920s.

THE CYCLONE OF 1876

The following harrowing account, by a sub-inspector of Police, Denonath Sircar, of Dowlutkhan Station, is of a cyclone and storm-surge that hit East Bengal on 31 October 1876.

'I was present at the [police] station on the night of the 31st October when the storm commenced. On the evening it commenced to blow from the east; at about 10 pm it began to blow with great force from the north-east. The station-house was then blown down. I took shelter behind the lock-up, where I gathered some of the prisoners who were there together before me, surrounded with a few constables. At about 11 pm a small house belonging to a mooktar caught fire. Our attention was directed in that quarter, when we suddenly found that water was gradually rising under our feet. Then suddenly we saw the water rushing towards us between the space of the lock-up and the guardhouse. When we saw this, we lost all hope. I told all the men to try and save themselves for the water in this interval had risen up to our waist. I attempted to go on the top of the roof of the guard-house, but was unable to go there on account of the great rush of the water, and I was drifted away by the stream inside the jail from whence with great difficulty some of us scrambled up on top of the prisoners' work-shed. The space between the lock-up and the guard-room was about three or four cubits, but such was the force of the water there that although three or four of us joined hands and attempted to force ourselves onwards to the guard-house, yet with all our strength we could not do so but were drifted down. The water began even to rise up to the work-shed roof, where we had perched ourselves. It rose so rapidly that the roof was carried along by the stream. We were about six or seven of us who held on to the roof which was even carried over some trees. The storm-waves were something dreadful. It came with great force and took away parts of the roof into different directions when we all were thrown into the water and got separated. I began to swim and was drifted away by the force of the rush of the water towards the south, when a half drowned "Balam" boat came before me and about two or three persons amongst whom was a prisoner who was also swimming, laid hold of it. Just as we had scrambled up the boat, a thatched roof belonging to some house was drifted against the boat with great force by the storm-wave. It struck several of us. The boat in the meanwhile began to sink, and we all had to take to the water and were drifted away, each in different directions. I found a large "madar" tree floating before me and laid hold of it. This was drifted into a garden full of mango, cocoanut and betelnut trees. I was, however, obliged to relinquish my hold, as the madar tree was full of thorns, and each time that it rose with the waves and brushed against my side, the thorns pricked my sides, hands and feet. After I let go the madar tree, I was drifted inside the garden, where I held the branch of a broken mango tree and stuck on to it there and retained my hold with the greatest difficulty till fair morning. I then sounded the depth of the water with a small piece of bamboo which was floating near me. The depth was 6 cubits (9 feet).'

ever known. The estimate made by citizens of Galveston was that 4000 houses . . . have been destroyed . . . the city is a complete wreck.'

The entire front page of the paper was devoted to the story, with more inside and on following days. Reading the whole account one is numbed by the repetition of tales of woe; for once, however, the maligned art of newspaper headline writing came into its own, with no need for sensationalism. The literal truth of the disaster is encapsulated in the headlines from that 10 September front page:

—GALVESTON WRECKED BY THE STORM.
—THOUSANDS OF LIVES LOST IN SOUTHERN TEXAS.
—THE ISLAND CITY ONE MASS OF DEBRIS, WITH FEW BUILDINGS INTACT.
—REFUGEES MAKE THEIR WAY TO THE MAINLAND AT GREAT RISK.
—TERRIBLE STORY OF THE HAVOC WROUGHT BY WIND AND WATER.
—HUNDREDS OF BODIES SEEN FLOATING IN THE BAY AND ON THE BEACH.
—EFFORTS TO REACH THE CITY HAVE SO FAR BEEN UNSUCCESSFUL.
—INHABITANTS IN A TERRIBLE PLIGHT, WITHOUT WATER, FOOD OR LIGHT.
—MANY SMALLER TOWNS NEAR THE COAST SUFFER — HOUSES DEMOLISHED AND PEOPLE KILLED.

We have one final example of the impact of a hurricane at sea: in 1944 when the strength and power of war fleets was at its height, a typhoon off the Philippines hammered Task Force 38 of the US Third Fleet, with equally dramatic results. Winds reaching 142 mph (227 kph) caught the Task Force unprepared and in the act of refuelling, with many ships riding light in the water and 90 vessels scattered across 3000 square miles (8000 sq km) of the Pacific Ocean.

An eyewitness described the results in these terms:

'Except in the case of the battleships, all semblance of formation had been lost. Every ship was laboring heavily; hardly any two were in visual contact; many lay dead, rolling in the trough of the sea; planes were crashing and burning on the light carriers. From the islands of the carriers and the pilot houses of destroyers sailors peered out on such a scene as they had never witnessed before, and hope never to see again. The weather was so thick and dirty that sea and sky seemed fused in one aqueous element. At times the rain was so heavy that visibility was limited to three feet, and the wind so powerful that to venture out on the flight deck a sailor had to wriggle on his belly. Occasionally the storm-wrack

A house at Bonnet Shores, Rhode Island, with its roof torn off after being struck by Hurricane Carol's 135 mph (216 kph) winds in August, 1954.

THE FLOODING OF PARIS

The floods that swamped Paris in January 1910 were the worst in two centuries. For two rain-swept weeks, the Seine rose steadily. By the 27th, 30,000 were homeless. The next day, along the Quai du Louvre, the Seine lapped at the top of its retaining walls, three feet above the road, while hundreds of Parisians banked them up with sandbags. Troops, with orders to shoot marauders, requisitioned 500 boats and evacuated families, sometimes forcibly. Only on the 29th, with half the city underwater, did the flood begin to recede.

CRUE DE LA SEINE   PARIS - Palais d'Orsay

A flooded street littered with books.

2 INONDATIONS DE PARIS (Janvier 1910). — La Rue Saint-Charles. — I. L.

Left: Evacuating flooded buildings.

Right: The flood near the Eiffel Tower.

Evacuations in central Paris.

The flight deck and side of USS *Hornet*, ripped and buckled by raging seas during a typhoon near Okinawa in June 1945.

parted for a moment, revealing escort carriers crazily rising up on their fantails or plunging bow under, destroyers rolling drunkenly in hundred-degree arcs or beaten down on one side. The big carriers lost no planes, but the extent of their rolls may be gauged by the fact that *Hancock*'s flight deck, 57 feet above her water line, scooped up green water.'

In all, the fleet lost three destroyers, 146 aircraft and 790 men, while an additional 18 ships were severely damaged and many others needed some repairs; the Allied plans for the war in the Pacific had to be modified to take account of this weakening of sea forces. Even 20th century fleets can be damaged as much by the force of the weather as by enemy action—so it is hardly surprising that some military minds have pondered on the possibility of steering hurricanes towards an enemy.

Down the years the story is much the same and it will remain so. Our civilization is helpless in the face of a hurricane, and the best we can hope for is to get warning of its coming and run away in time to save our lives, if not our property. The tales

outlined here, though they come in many cases from another century, are still relevant to us today, serving to stress that violence is the natural result of the workings of the atmosphere.

But at least hurricanes do not strike everywhere in the world, and not usually anywhere with the frequency of the four storms in one year that ran through Texas in 1886. Most people most of the time only have to worry about the lesser and more localized aspects of weather force.

Tornadoes deserve a special mention, being some kind of kin to hurricanes, although no one yet understands the exact relationship between the two. The trouble with twisters—as tornadoes are often known—is that they can strike rapidly and unexpectedly, and often in flocks. This was the case on Palm Sunday, 11 April 1965, when Indiana was the hardest hit of six US States located in the 'tornado belt,' with 91 people killed in that State alone. More than 100 homes and a shopping plaza were wrecked in one small area, two blocks by five blocks; a Greyhound bus was flipped over by one

A SURVIVOR'S TALE

Here is one of the many hundreds of terrifying and surreal experiences undergone by survivors of tornadoes. This account is taken from the *Chicago Daily Tribune* of Saturday 21 March 1925:

'Mrs Judith Cox, wife of a Missouri Pacific workman, was in a Gorham restaurant visiting Miss Mary Clark and Miss Lulu Moschenrose when the sky suddenly darkened.

"It began to rain and I thought I would go home," said Mrs Cox. "I opened the door and saw a great wall that seemed to be smoke, driving in front of it white billows that looked like steam. There was a deep roar, like a train, but many, many times louder.

"The air was full of everything—boards, branches of trees, pans, stoves, all churning around together. I saw whole sides of houses rolling along near the ground.

"It seemed to me that I must reach my two children in school, and I opened the door again, bent my head down against the wind and started out. Then the storm hit me. I was blown back into the restaurant and against the stove. The building rocked back and forth and then it began to fall in. Fire flashed in great puffs from the stove.

"I tried to get away from it. I was afraid I would be burned to death. But the wind blew me back again against it. Then the walls fell in. The roof fell. Something hit me on the head.

"How long I was unconscious I don't know. When I came to I was buried under boards and timbers. Near me was the body of a red cow which seemed to be holding some of the weight off of me.

"Then came Joe Moschenrose, the butcher, looking for his sister. He saw me, lifted some of the heavy boards, helped the cow up and pulled me out. I got up and looked around. There, on the floor, white in death, was Lulu, with a great wound in her head.

"I started for the school. I found my own raincoat down the street hanging on a twisted pile of planking. I was wearing it when the storm struck. I put my hand in the pocket. There was my husband's pay check.

"There was a great crowd about the school. Children were screaming and crying. Mothers and fathers were weeping silently. But everybody was trying to dig out their own children. I found mine. They were both hurt, but alive." '

twister; and in Iowa a whole farmhouse was carried 60 feet (18 m) into the air before crashing back to the ground. Overall the death toll from 37 tornadoes on that day of disaster reached more than 250 and damage totalled more than $250 million.

One eyewitness report sums up the power of these ferocious funnels of wind. The report was one of many carried in the *Washington Post* on 13 April:

'Deanna Wyant, 19, was entertaining a boy friend, Don Dalton, 20, in her family's second floor apartment when her mother phoned to say that she had heard a tornado warning on the radio.

'"We'd better hurry," Deanna said. The tornado hit as they reached the door.

'Both were lifted off their feet. "We just seemed to fly around the room," Deanna said.

'"Don saved my life," the girl said. "He held me down and covered me with his body. Then the ceiling collapsed."

'When she stood up she found that the house had disintegrated around them. They were on the foundations.

'"I looked down at Don and his eyes were closed," she recalled later. "I thought he was dead and ran into the street screaming.

'"The wind was still blowing. I held on to a tree. I saw the dark cloud moving away and then the sky seemed to light up." '

This is a typical account. Basically the twisting winds of a tornado revolve around a central core in which pressure is so low that when it touches a house the building may explode from the pressure of air inside, or be lifted bodily, like the Kansas farmhouse of *The Wizard of Oz*, into the air. Such a force easily lifts lesser objects, like branches, trees, and even people. Yet a few people have seen the 'eye' of a tornado funnel pass right over them without being harmed. This may occur as a result of the peculiar behavior of twisters, which sometimes reach down from the clouds without touching the ground. The classic report is that of a Kansas farmer, Will Keller, who saw a tornado approaching on 22 June 1928. He dived into his cyclone cellar and turned to close the door:

'As I paused to look I saw that the lower end which had been sweeping the ground

The extraordinary consequence of a tornado in Flint, Michigan in May 1956: the wind apparently bent the glass from its frame, sucked the curtain through and then allowed the glass to spring back into position.

one half mile, as best I could judge under the circumstances. The walls of this opening were of rotating clouds and the whole was made brilliantly visible by constant flashes of lightning which zigzagged from side to side. Had it not been for the lightning I could not have seen the opening, not any distance up into it anyway.

'Around the lower rim of the great vortex small tornadoes were constantly forming and breaking away. These looked like tails as they writhed their way around the end of the funnel. It was these that made the hissing noise.

'I noticed that the direction of rotation of the great whirl was anticlockwise, but the small twisters rotated both ways— some one way and some another.

'The opening was entirely hollow except for something which I could not exactly make out, but suppose that it was a detached wind cloud.'

How do tornadoes form? The details are still not terribly clear, but one thing is sure —they need a supply of moist, warm rising air to start the updraft that combines with spinning winds to cause the devastation. And regardless of any natural changes in the weather or of the very small influence of mankind so far on the climate in general, this is something that man's activities do provide. Damp, rising air is much more common over urban areas than open country, and urbanization continues apace. This almost certainly is one reason why the annual average number of tornado sightings in the US for the 20 years ending 1969 was 581, while for the 20 years ending 1949 the equivalent number was only 162. Of course radar and other improvements in weather monitoring ensure that most tornadoes are spotted today while many may have slipped through the net before. But that alone cannot account for this almost fourfold increase. In 1970 alone 650 tornadoes were sighted in the US; all the evidence is that numbers certainly have increased compared with a few decades ago.

Other features of the weather much more 'ordinary' than floods, hurricanes or tornadoes can provide a powerful local impact —lightning for instance. Meteorologists have calculated that lightning occurs all over the Earth at a rate of 6000 strokes a minute, so it is hardly news. Most deaths from lightning are lone individuals, con-

was beginning to rise. I knew what that meant, so I kept my position. I knew that I was comparatively safe and I knew that if the tornado again dipped I could drop down and close the door before any harm could be done.

'Steadily the tornado came on, the end gradually rising above the ground. I could have stood there only a few seconds but so impressed was I with what was going on that it seemed a long time. At last the great shaggy end of the funnel hung directly overhead. Everything was as still as death. There was a strong gassy odor and it seemed that I could not breathe. There was a screaming, hissing sound coming directly from the end of the funnel. I looked up and to my astonishment I saw right up into the heart of the tornado. There was a circular opening in the center of the funnel, about 50 or 100 feet in diameter, and extending straight upward for a distance of at least sequently the impact is not massive in any one case. Yet the annual death toll from lightning in the US exceeds 600, and injuries run above 1500 a year—both figures are several times larger than the corresponding annual totals for hurricanes and tornadoes in the US.

The world's living expert on lightning, from first-hand experience, must be former US Marine Corps pilot William Rankin, who baled out of his fighter at an altitude of 47,000 feet (14,326 m)—9 miles (14 km)—and fell into the middle of a thunderstorm. His parachute was set to open at 10,000 feet (3048 m), and in normal circumstances he would have fallen from there to the ground in a few minutes. But the violent winds of the thunderstorm bounced him up and down like the ping-pong ball on a jet of water at a shooting gallery, for three quarters of an hour before letting him go. All the while he was surrounded by lightning and deafened by giant thunderclaps:

'I was blown up and down as much as 6000 feet at a time. It went on for a long time, like being on a very fast elevator, with strong blasts of compressed air hitting you. Once when a violent blast of air sent me careering up into the chute and I could feel the cold, wet nylon collapsing about me, I was sure the chute would never blossom again. But, by some miracle, I fell back and the chute *did* recover its billow.

'The wind had savage allies. The first clap of thunder came as a deafening explosion that literally shook my teeth. I didn't *hear* the thunder, I actually *felt* it—an almost unbearable physical experience. If it had not been for my helmet, the explosions might have shattered my eardrums.

'I saw lightning all around me in every shape imaginable. When very close, it appeared mainly as a huge, bluish sheet several feet thick. It was raining so torrentially that I thought I would drown in midair. Several times I held my breath, fearing that otherwise I might inhale quarts of water.'

THE WIDECOMBE FIREBALL

One of the most macabre tragedies associated with lightning occurred in an English West Country village of Widecombe in Devon. The disaster struck on Sunday, 21 October 1638. The congregation was gathered in the church and the vicar had just begun the service when suddenly the sky went black and the building was hit by wind and lightning of the utmost violence. A ball of fire moved through the church and then burst with a thunderous explosion, 'which so much affrighted the whole Congregation that the most part of them fell downe into their seates, and some upon their knees, some on their faces, and some upon one another, with a great cry of burning and scalding they all giving up themselves for dead.' People were snatched from the pews and whirled about. Some were set down completely unharmed, others were dashed against walls and pillars. A man's head 'was cloven, his skull rent into three pieces, and his braines throwne upon the ground whole, and the hair of his head, through the violence of the blow at first given him, did sticke fast unto the pillar or wall of the church; so that hee perished there most lamentably.'

A Mrs Ditford had 'her gowne, two wastecoates, and linnen next her body, burned cleane off; and her back also very grievously downe to her waste burned and scalded, and so exceedingly afflicted thereby, shee could neither stand nor goe without helpe, being lead out of the church.' Altogether four were killed and 56 injured.

All this took place in a few seconds and while those who were left alive were still terror-struck, the church was filled with 'a very thick mist, with smother, smoake and smell.' The latter, reminiscent of brimstone, came from the lightning and bursting fireball, but to the 17th-century worshippers it was the signature of the Devil himself.

Richard Hill, the village schoolmaster at the time, wrote a poem to commemorate the event. His doggerel is still displayed on boards in the church.

Some had their skin all over scorched, yet no harm to their clothes
One man had money in his purse which melted was in part. . . .
The church within so filled was with timber stones and fire
That scarce a vacant place was seen in church or in the choir.

Lightning is literally a giant electric spark; the thunder results from a sudden increase in pressure as the air is heated by the literally explosive passage of the electric discharge. The pressure wave expands and is sensed as sound. But just how giant electric discharges are built up in storm clouds is not yet certain, though it is clear that the process is associated with the production of frozen water droplets—soft hail—falling through the cloud. Back in 1955 British meteorologist B J Mason—now Director-General of the UK Meteorological Office—said 'it is one thing to have a plausible theory [of lightning], and another to prove it beyond all reasonable doubt. There is still a long way to go.' Twenty-five years later, while the ice drop theory seems to be accepted as an explanation of lightning production in freezing clouds, meteorologists remain baffled by the presence of lightning in warm clouds, and the UK Meteorological Office's book *Elementary Meteorology* admits that 'a coherent theory for the electrification of warm clouds has yet to be found.' So the puzzle of how lightning occurs remains to be completely resolved.

As well as being implicated in at least some processes by which lightning is produced, hail itself is a major problem. Agriculture is extremely vulnerable to this shrapnel from the sky which causes losses of around $400 (£200) million a year in the US, according to official Department of Agriculture figures. Small wonder that intense efforts have been made from time to time to turn the hail into rain by seeding storm clouds, with the Russians, in particular going so far as to shoot anti-aircraft guns at the clouds!

If anyone should think it an extreme reaction to a bit of unfavorable weather, ponder some of the information given in the *Guiness Book of Weather Facts and Feats*:

—Hailstones as large as cricket balls fell in Northern India in 1888, killing 246 people and 1600 animals.

—Similar sized hailstones rained on Dallas, Texas, on 8 May 1926, causing $2 million damage in 15 minutes.

—A hailstorm in China in June 1932 killed 200 people.

—Half-pound hailstones fell on Durban, South Africa, on 17 November 1949 causing £500,000 damage.

—India was battered again on 27 May 1959

Lightning flickers in a storm over Spain, showing flashes between air-pockets of different electrical charge as well as between air and ground.

BOMBARDMENTS OF ICE

One of the most surprisingly destructive of phenomena is hail. Hail insurance in the US amounts to over a billion dollars a year. Hailstones, which are usually less than one half inch (13 mm) in diameter, can occasionally reach baseball size.

The damage caused by large hailstones is almost unbelievable. On 14 July 1953 such a hailstorm swept over the Alberta Province of Canada covering a path some 140 miles (224 km) long and 5 miles (8 km) wide. The hailstones were as large as golf balls, some even larger. The storm was accompanied by winds up to 75 mph (120 kph).

Allen G Smith, biologist of the US Fish and Wildlife Service, wrote: 'Grasses and herbs were shredded beyond recognition

occurred in an areas where there are regular aerial surveys of wildfowl.

On 18 July another severe hailstorm occurred in the same area, this time killing an estimated 28,000 ducks and ducklings.

The most deadly hailstorm of which there is authentic record burst over the Moradabad Beheri districts of India on 30 April 1888. Two hundred and forty-six people were killed. Some were pounded to death, but the majority were knocked down by stones and wind, buried under drifts, and died of cold and exposure. More than 1600 head of cattle, sheep and goats were killed.

An unsigned eyewitness report in *The Times of India* of Monday 7 May 1888, reported the largest hailstones known to

Peach-sized hailstones that fell in Queenstown, South Africa in 1879.

and beaten into the earth. Trees and shrubs were stripped of all leaves and small branches and the bark on one side of the larger trees had been torn away or deeply gouged by hailstones. Plants growing in waters of the potholes and lakes were reduced to nondescript pulp. Emergent vegetation had disappeared, destroyed and beaten under the water's surface by the weight of the hail. Ponds that had been choked with grasses, sedges, cattails, and bullrush since June, were stripped of all plant growth.'

Songbirds, hawks, owls and other birds were killed by the thousand. The number of ducks killed—36,000—was estimated with reasonable accuracy because the hailstorm

date: 'Incredible as it may seem, one picked up in the hospital garden in the fort weighed one-and-a-half pounds. More extraordinary still, another hailstone secured near the telegraph office was of the size of an average melon, and turned the scale at two pounds. These stones were weighed in the presence of witnesses by two gentlemen of unquestionable veracity. . . . The fall for about two minutes presented the appearance of a shower of lumps of ice, most of which smashed on coming in contact with the earth, only those which fell into soft earth having been secured intact. The shape of the stones generally was a flat oval, very few being round like ordinary hail.'

A field of corn stripped by hailstones

Hailstones six inches in circumference in Calcutta, April 1975.

with 8-inch (20-cm) diameter hailstones which caused 15-inch (38-cm) diameter holes in an aircraft.

What else can 'ordinary' weather bring to plague us? Some hazards are now less than before, as in the case of the killing London 'smogs' (fog polluted by industrial smoke) which were a feature of the decades up to the 1950s, but have now vanished due to clean-air legislation (though other cities such as Los Angeles have yet to learn the lesson).

Avalanches continue to make news somewhere every year, and the potential for disaster here can be gauged from one example, that of the cascade of four million tons of ice and snow down from the peak (22,205 feet [6768 m] high) of Nevado de Huascaran in Peru. Roaring down a valley, this avalanche swept up rocks and mud while travelling a total of 11 miles (18 km) at 60 mph (96 kph) sweeping into oblivion one town, seven villages and 3500 people in just over ten minutes.

Equally devastating, though slightly less sudden in their onset, are the storm surges which can occur anywhere that a funnelling neck of water exists, such as in the classic case of the North Sea between Britain and Europe. When the winds blow strongly down the funnel and combine with high tide, water literally piles up in the 'neck' (in that case, the English Channel) and floods the surrounding land. The flat country of East Anglia, the Thames Estuary and London, and the low-lying region of Holland have been repeatedly battered in this way; in 1953, for example, 307 people died in England in such a surge and 30,000 were made homeless, while in Holland dykes collapsed, 1800 drowned and 50,000 were evacuated. Such a surge is certain to come again, and although the Thames is now better protected by new flood barriers, East Anglia and Holland are still at the mercy of the storm surge.

One major element has been omitted from this roll call of disasters—the direct effect of severe winters. This is not because we know little about such events—quite the reverse. The saga of changing severity of winters over the centuries provides us with the best way of getting an understanding of broad changes in the working of the atmosphere, and it is a story that demands its own chapter.

A whirling pillar of dust moves across Texas, 1968.

T E POWER OF T E TWISTER

A tornado must rank as the most terrifying of all natural phenomena. Winds that are estimated to reach up to 500 mph (800 kph) encircle a low pressure area that may be less than 100 yards across. If a house withstands the initial impact, the sudden lack of pressure at the tornado's eye may cause the house to explode. Cars may be blown along like tumbleweed and people tossed into the air. Moreover, tornadoes are surprisingly common. In 1973 the US recorded 1000 of them. The following year, on just one day—4 April—10 eastern States were ravaged by a regiment of 90 tornadoes.

The whirling funnel cloud appears to grow vertically or slantwise down from a dark, heavy cumulonimbus as moisture cools, expanding rapidly and sucking up air from below (but how exactly they form and what powers them is still a mystery). Sweeping along at 10–50 mph (16–80 kph), their bases are held back by friction, although occasionally they are clear of the ground. After a few miles, the twisters withdraw into the clouds from which they sprang.

A tornado in the process of formation over Texas.

A waterspout hits Spain's Costa Brava coastline on 2 September 1965.

A waterspout off Florida.

A dust-devil, a tornado in miniature, in Kenya.

The swathe of damage after
a tornado has swept through
Sheppard Air Force Base,
Wichita Falls, Texas in
April 1964.

A wooden post plunged into the ground and snapped off by a tornado.

4: THE MESSAGE OF THE PAST

The fluctuations of weather conditions from day to day and month to month conceal longer term climatic patterns that emerge only from a re-interpretation of historical evidence from a scientific point of view.

This early 17th-century Dutch skating scene by Hendrick Avercamp was one of many done by Dutch painters of this popular subject – popular because, as the Little Ice Age progressed, the bitter cold made thick ice a regular feature of every winter.

The National Gallery

The most recent great Ice Age ended in round terms about 10,000 years ago. During the great cold millennia before that, the ice had acted as an unwitting agent in the rise of mankind to dominance in the high latitudes of our planet, making conditions so harsh that only the most cunning species could survive and develop. From those harsh times only man and the wolf emerged triumphant; man, however, had the flexibility to continue to adapt to improving climatic conditions, so that civilization burst forth in the more pleasant millennia that followed while the wolf took his place at man's side, domesticated as the ancestor of the dog. In the next chapter, we shall look at the broad sweep of climatic changes, those which brought about the Ice Age which proved so beneficial to prehistoric man, and those which may bring the next Ice Age, which may prove less beneficial to modern, softer, civilized man. Here, though, I wish to look at the way in which vagaries of weather and climate have helped or hindered the development of civilization during that brief span of 10,000 years since things changed noticeably for the better.

The ups and downs have been dramatic by any standard except that of the transition out of the full Ice Age itself. Warming after the great glaciation brought such a melting that sea level rose to ten feet (three meters) above its present height by about 2000 BC, with effects that may linger on in folklore as the many tales of a great flood in prehistoric times. The total *rise* in sea level, of course, was much greater than ten feet (three meters) since it started out from much below the present level—before, so much water was locked up in ice that the English Channel was dry land. The warming brought wetter weather than we know today to much of northern Africa, including the Sahara region, and the deserts and coastal zones of the Near East—so it is hardly surprising, in climatic terms, that the early civilizations should have grown up in these warm, moist regions.

But it did not last. The millennium immediately before Christ was considerably colder (the 'Iron Age Cold Epoch'), but also even wetter in the north, encouraging the spread of great gloomy forests across what is now Russia. In the Mediterranean, the climate grew both cooler and drier, restricting the range over which Roman farm-

ers could grow vines and olives. As the seesaw swung back, things improved again for farmers in the temperate and Mediterranean zones, with a little 'climatic optimum' peaking between 1000 and 1200 AD encouraging the spread of Norse colonies across the Northern Atlantic. This also allowed vines to be cultivated as much as 5° farther north than before and up to over 600 feet (200 meters) higher above sea level, and generally provided a boost for the activities of mankind's many flourishing local civilizations.

This illustration of an English wine harvest, taken from the Peterborough Psalter of the mid-13th century, is evidence of the warm spell that preceded the onset of the Little Ice Age.

Once again, though, the seesaw tilted to swing the world back into cold so severe that the period from about 1430 to 1850 has been dubbed the 'Little Ice Age.' Then farmers had to struggle against violent extremes of weather; Norse colonies in the north were destroyed by the encroaching cold; forests across Europe declined dramatically; and vine cultivation, among other things, became once again a predominantly Mediterranean activity.

Since 1850 the climate has improved, becoming both warmer and more stable, although still falling some way short of the optimum. In the past decade or so, there has been a hint that this brief lull may be over, with more violent extremes of weather and a general cooling indicated. Has the Little Ice Age really ended? What will happen to us if it has not—or even if some other swing of the seesaw brings conditions never encountered in a human lifetime? These questions can only be answered with the aid of hindsight, the message from the past. And the message is far from being an encouraging one for a heavily populated world with few reserves of food.

The evidence for all these changes comes from a variety of sources. Sometimes it is straightforwardly historical, as in the case of Roman writings which tell us about the extent of vineyards and their success—or failure; at other times climatologists have to rely on what are called 'proxy data,' the changing thickness of the annual rings laid down by trees, the preserved pollen of different species of plants left in layers of sediments in lake beds, or the record in the sands and rocks of shorelines of the rise and fall of sea or lake levels. One thing emerges very persuasively from all these records, even when the root causes of the long term changes in the weather are not clear. This is that during cooling phases of climatic shift, by and large, the whole pattern of circulation around the poles (described in Chapter 2) expands, squeezing climatic zones more tightly about the equator and causing the jet stream and its associated depressions to zigzag more widely over the temperate zone.

Such an expansion of the 'circumpolar vortex' has clear implications for particular regions of the globe. One is that by preventing the northward spread of moist air from the Gulf of Mexico, the depressions would cause droughts in the regions of central North America in the 'rain shadow' of the Rockies. This clearcut 'prediction' encouraged US climatologist Professor Reid Bryson of the University of Wisconsin at Madison to enlist the aid of expert archeologists to investigate just what happened in that region at the time of the great global cooling from the 13th century onwards.

The team knew of the existence of several abandoned Amerindian villages in the region of North America that is now northwestern Iowa, and knew that these villages had been inhabited by members of a farming and hunting civilization about 1200 AD. What happened to cause the villages to be abandoned? Today the area has about 25 inches (64 cm) of rain per year, produces good crops of corn and soya beans, and is reasonably comfortable for farmers. A drop of 25 percent in rainfall, however, would cause severe problems for agriculture—and if that is what happened about 800 years ago as the circumpolar vortex expanded, archeologists were sure that they would find the tell-tale evidence in the debris left behind by the Mill Creek Indians. At the same time the climate experts on the team looked to analyze different kinds of pollen from the plants that were around 800 years ago, pollen scattered and left to reveal the vegetation that was dominant when the Indian culture flourished.

Both lines of attack came up with the same result, graphically described by Professor Bryson in his book *Climates of Hunger*. After about 1200 AD (painstakingly dated using the most modern techniques, including radiocarbon dating) the way of life of the Indians changed, and the nature of the countryside around them changed. There were fewer trees, indicating a decline in rainfall, and a shift in favor of the kinds of short grass that can survive in climates drier than those needed by tall grass and corn. A change in the diet of the inhabitants of the Mill Creek region, showing up in a decline in the variety of bones found in their rubbish dumps, indicated a shortage of game, with a change in emphasis from deer to bison. Whereas deer need moisture and forests, of course, bison can cope better with drier conditions and open grassland.

All the pieces fitted together and the message is clear. In the words used by Bryson and his colleague Thomas Murray:

The forbidding Tassili Plateau as it is today.

Two prehistoric hunters etched on the walls of a shallow cave.

THE SAHARA'S VANISHED GREENERY

The Sahara had not always been a desert. Over the last two million years, it has fluctuated several times between aridity and greenness. For several millennia BC, hunters and herders left vivid evidence of the changes in Saharan climate in thousands of rock paintings, which can still be seen in the mountainous massifs, particularly in the Tassili n Ajjer Plateau.

It is thought there were three main periods of Saharan pre-history. Before 5000 BC the inhabitants were hunters; from 4000 BC to 2000 BC, they were pastoralists with large herds of cattle; and about 1200 BC, when the Sahara began to dry out and camels appeared, the Saharan peoples began to migrate. If ice ever returns to higher latitudes, the Sahara may one day flourish again, and provide rich supplies of grain, meat and milk.

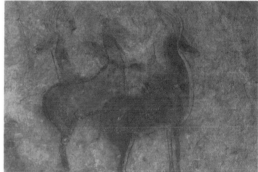

Two antelopes, creatures of the grassy plains.

Cattle: evidence of a farming economy.

A mouflon, a wild sheep, still seen in the area.

'The Mill Creek farmers, and their contemporaries throughout the plains, were not victims of just the Biblical seven years of famine, or even of a human generation of bad years. The changed climate that brought the downfall of the plains farmers probably lasted about 200 years. . . . The final decline of the Mill Creek people came just before the westerlies changed back again and more rains came to northwestern Iowa . . . how would we, the civilization of 20th-century plains corn farmers, have done?'

This is a key consideration in the world today, since as we shall see later a disproportionate amount of vital world food comes from just these same plains of North America. Two hundred years' drought in this breadbasket of the world hardly bears thinking about, yet the message from the past is that just such a drought can happen.

Bryson's studies also help us to understand the decline of an even greater civilization thousands of years earlier and thousands of miles away. Covering the boundary between what is now Pakistan and what is now India, a great civilization based on the Indus river grew up some 4500 years ago and lasted for about 1000 years. In round

terms the end of the Indus civilization and a period of drought in the region, with repeated failure of the life-giving monsoons, coincided with the shift farther north out of the climatic optimum and into the cold epoch of the Iron Age. Once again the cooling pushed the climatic zones towards the equator, with very pronounced effects in this critical region at the northern limit of the monsoon winds. Once again both climatic studies and archeological data have combined to spell out the story in parallel steps. And once again the implications are decidedly gloomy for 20th century mankind, with the same region today still dependent on the monsoons, housing a rapidly growing population, and being one of political tension between two not-very-friendly neighboring states.

This time, however, the scope of the disaster and its very long-lasting after-effects carry another warning for mankind. As far as the archeologists can tell, the inhabitants of the Indus civilization, centered on the two great cities of Harappa and Mohenjo-Daro, contributed to their own downfall by bad farming practices which changed conditions in the Indus valley so drastically

Two views of the same area – the Rhône Glacier – show the differences that a century can bring to ice cover. The painting on the left was done in 1857; the picture on the right was taken in 1960.

that, with the extra push of a climatic shift as well, a partly man-made desert was produced'. In recent years the desert has been growing, after experiencing waves of growth and retreat in the past 3500 years. Yet again overgrazing and destruction of forests by man have encouraged the dangerous trend; and yet again a natural climatic shift may be emphasizing the detrimental influence of man's activities.

The worst thing that has happened in climatic terms during historical times was the Little Ice Age. Since that spell of severe weather dominated the past 1000 years, any prudent planning ought to take account of the possibility that something similar may return. But in fact the great explosion of what has become a global society has occurred as conditions improved after about 1850, and naturally enough we tend to think of 'normal' weather and climate as the kind we have experienced in our own lifetimes. The disasters of 1976–78, discussed in Chapter 1, point up the dangers of this complacency, and have begun to change attitudes about what really is 'normal' in terms of what the weather can do to us. But has the warning come too

late? And, if a reversion to the Little Ice Age is possible, just what would that imply?

What matters most to us is the variability of weather from year to year or decade to decade—the occurrence of extremes, like the US winter of 1978 or the English summer of 1976. Averages do not tell the whole story by any means, and the average temperature over the whole year in an Ice Age is probably only about 9°F (5°C) below the global annual average today— much less than the day-to-day variations we are used to dealing with. Geographical averages can also be misleading; remember that in 1977 the US Southwest suffered severe drought while the Northeast was buried deep in snow, so that over the whole country the 'average' precipitation was far from extreme. No, rather than averages, it is the frequency of extremes that matters to the farmer—the late frosts in spring, the number of drought years in a decade, the occurrence of violent storms, and so on. This is why the discovery that a cooling of the globe, and expansion of the circumpolar vortex, bringing increased variability and a climate of extremes to the temperate zones, is so important.

The Frost Fair of 1683: coaches, horse-drawn sledges, and a 'tent city.'

Stalls and games on the frozen Thames, January 1749.

THE FROZEN THAMES

One example of the way historical studies can help the climatologist is provided by the history of the River Thames over the past nine centuries. Droughts are revealed by stories of years such as 1114, when in October the river was so low that children could wade across it at London, and of 1325 and 1326, when tidal salt water penetrated far up river.

The Little Ice Age, worst in London during the 17th century, brought extreme variations of weather—and not just a run of continuing cold; some years were hit by severe drought, as in 1666 when the tinder-dry condition of the wooden houses provided fuel for the Great Fire of London. Nevertheless, the freezing winters stand out most obviously from the historical record. The years when the Thames froze at London provide the most clearcut indications of the way the Little Ice Age hit England.

Up to about 1000 AD the available records tell us that the Thames only froze eight times, less than once in a hundred years. The hard winter of 1149–50 marks the beginning of a period when such events became more common, while at the same time the historical records become more reliable. In that winter, men were able to cross the frozen river on horseback. There was another hard frost that covered the river with ice only half a century later, in 1204–05. In 1209 the

The Frost Fair of 1814: swings, side-shows and food stalls.

old London Bridge was completed, which enabled ice to form more easily, piling up against the bridge and freezing across the river.

In 1269–70 the frozen river obstructed water traffic so far downstream that goods from the Channel ports had to travel overland—very much a last resort, given the frightful conditions of the roads. And from Christmas 1281 until March 1282 the river was frozen solidly enough to be used as a highway by pedestrians crossing from one bank to the other.

Then came a brief respite before the full onset of the Little Ice Age, with no more freeze-ups in the 14th century. From 1407–08 to 1564–65, however, the river froze six times, with horses and carts being driven across on several occasions and both Henry VIII and Elizabeth I venturing on to the ice. Football was played on the river in 1564–65, but its heyday as a winter attraction came in the 17th century, with the frequent establishment of 'Frost Fairs' —tent cities that sprang up offering various kinds of amusement and refreshment for the populace. The first of these was in 1607–08, others in 1620–21 and 1662–63. But the greatest of them all was in 1683–84. Another monarch, Charles II, visited this river 'city,' built on ice 11 inches thick which stayed solid for two months. Another Frost Fair was held in 1688–89.

In all, there were ten winters in the 17th century when the river froze solid. Another ten great freezes occurred between 1708–09 and 1813–14, when the last Frost Fair was held. It was rather a poor affair lasting only a few days.

'The ice,' the *Times* reported on 2 February 'from its roughness and inequalities, is totally unfit for amusement,' although the following day, 3 February, *The Morning Post* reported, 'An elephant on the ice . . . Yesterday a very fine elephant crossed the Thames a little below Blackfriars Bridge; the singularity of such an animal on the ice attracted a great concourse, who accompanied him to the Olympic Theatre, where he was ushered into his new apartments in the presence of at least five thousand spectators.' The ice gave way on 6 February and the River Thames has not frozen since.

In 1831 the old London Bridge was destroyed, allowing the water to flow more freely; the climate began to improve; and man began to warm up the river with effluent from power stations and industry. The age of Frost Fairs is probably over for good, even if Little Ice Age conditions return.

The end of the Frost Fairs: London Bridge on 5 February 1814.

THE TELL-TALE TREES

Among the many techniques used by climatologists to study the weather of the past, two depend on the ways trees grow and reproduce.

During its life, a tree in a seasonal climate grows in annual spurts, adding successive layers of new wood each year which we see as annual rings in sections cut through logs or in tree stumps. At low latitudes with little seasonal variations of weather, the trees do not show this pattern; but where there are large temperature changes (as in Europe) or large rainfall changes, as in some tropical countries, the annual growth pattern occurs.

The first thing we can tell from the rings is the age of a tree, simply by counting backwards from the outermost layer, the one laid down most recently. But the rings also vary in width from one year to the next and, by and large, a wide ring means a good year, while a narrow ring means conditions were bad. High on a mountain, such as the Rockies of the southwestern US, 'bad' means that the growing season was cold; in the lowlands of a temperate country such as Britain, 'bad' generally means dry. For many trees in many parts of the world it is very difficult to unravel from studies of the changing widths of tree rings, the separate, and sometimes contradictory, influences of temperature and rainfall. But where this can be done—and the technique is getting better all the time—the results are spectacular.

The classic case is provided by the very long-lived bristlecone pine of the White Mountains of California. The oldest living

If we go back a thousand years to get a view of the circumstances leading up to the Little Ice Age of recent centuries, we find easy conditions at high latitudes which made for the success of the Norse people as travellers and conquerors. Iceland, Greenland and the North American continent felt the impact of the Norse as an ocean-going race while their brothers travelled inland from the Baltic Sea, following the great rivers into the heart of Russia and south into the Black Sea and Eastern Mediterranean.

But as the globe began to cool down and the change in climatic patterns which hit the Mill Creek Indians so hard became established, ice encroached upon the north-ern sea routes, agriculture failed in Greenland and the Norse colony died out as the Eskimos moved in from the north with their way of life, adapted to much colder conditions. The Baltic became much more icy for long periods of the year and even river navigation in the north became difficult, effectively cutting off the settlers from their original homelands.

It is hard to pin down a global definition of the dates which frame the Little Ice Age proper because the most extreme conditions hit different parts of the world in different centuries. Most severe conditions seem to have come first in the northern hemisphere and later in the southern, and there were things on Earth, some of these trees have been growing undisturbed for 4600 years. It would be outrageous to cut down such a tree, but 'dendrochronologists' and 'dendroclimatologists' — as researchers in this esoteric field are known—can extract a thin core running into the heart of the tree without doing it any harm. Even better, the characteristic patterns of broad and narrow annual rings in such living wood can be matched up with the outer layers of still older, dead wood from the same sites. Since all the trees suffered the same weather variations, they have the same growth patterns for the years when they were alive. The patterns can be built up in overlapping bands, and in this way, the bristlecone pine weather gauge has been extended back to 3551 BC (the date can be given exactly).

In their high mountains, the growth of these trees depends almost entirely on temperature. The tree-ring thermometer gives us a record of changing temperatures going back more than 5000 years. Only temperatures from one part of the globe, true; but as we have seen, these are part of the global trends, and from more recent weather changes climatologists have a good idea of how the California temperature changes tie in to the broader picture. To take just one example, the Little Ice Age had its counterpart in California, judging from these tree rings; since the rings are also narrow for many years in a cold period beginning about 3000 years ago, here is a firm indication that the world as a whole was cooler then than it has been in recent decades. So for more than five millennia we have a precise year by year indication of the changing climate.

Along with other plants, trees also provide indications of climatic patterns changing on the broader sweep of centuries, and going back even further in time. The tiny pollen grains scattered so profusely by the flowers of trees and other plants are spread by the wind so that many find their way into the mud of lake bottoms, where they are trapped. Accumulating sediment over the decades produces a layer in which the kind of pollen found at any particular depth indicates the plants that were alive in the region during the years the sediment at that depth was settling. Dated by the radioactive carbon-14 they contain, such pollen remains, by revealing the changing patterns of vegetation, tell us how the broad sweep of climate has varied. This is one of the best indicators of the long warm period, beginning about 10,000 years ago, when oak forests dominated a northwest Europe about 1°C (2°F) warmer than the temperatures of the 20th century.

California's sturdy, long-lived bristlecone pine (left) and the tree's tangle of roots (below).

also considerable differences in timing of Little Ice Age severity between Europe and America, China and Japan. Different experts have chosen different, necessarily arbitrary, dates for the start and end of the Little Ice Age, the starting dates ranging from 1300 AD to 1560, and the ending dates ranging from 1700 to the commonly chosen 1850, with a few climatologists arguing that the Little Ice Age has not yet really finished at all. For convenience, in very round terms, we can think of the three hundred years from 1550 to 1850 as typifying Little Ice Age conditions.

Although the various ups and downs of the weather were not exactly in time around the world, we can also choose Europe as a region particularly hard hit by the Little Ice Age, and as a center of the then-civilized world with good historical records for us to study to provide an idea of just what these changes meant in human terms. The historians provide a wealth of information but the climatologists must find ways of relating this to changes in temperature, rainfall and storminess. One very neat, if initially surprising, tool of the trade has turned out to be a study of the dates of the wine harvests in France and other parts of Europe made by the historian Emmanuel Le Roy Ladurie of the University of Paris.

Professor Ladurie realized that, since wine grapes are picked when ripe, and their ripeness depends very much on the weather while they were growing, such records ought to give a direct guide to the severity of summer weather over the years. The dates of the harvest in wine growing regions are important news kept in official registers, police records and so on, easily available to the historian. And, as a final check before committing himself and using such records as a guide to climatic changes, Ladurie used the existing temperature records of the 19th century for comparison against the wine harvest 'thermometer' of the same period. The result was accurate confirmation that the date of the wine harvest does indeed correspond closely to average temperatures. The later the harvest, the colder the summer has been—and the method is precise enough to give a good guide to just how cold the summer was.

One example from German records highlights the value of the technique. For the hundred years from 1453 to 1552, wine from the vineyards of western Germany produced almost equal numbers of 'good' and 'poor' vintages—the climate was playing no great tricks. Then from 1553 onwards the date of the harvest was later and the quality of the wine declined; for 50 years the weather was

THE FINDING OF THE FLOOD

The Biblical Flood was probably the most catastrophic of many floods that ravaged the Tigris–Euphrates civilizations between about 4000 and 3000 BC. The proof that there had been at least one major inundation was provided by the British archaeologist Sir Charles Leonard Woolley in 1929. 'Probing what seemed to be the earliest levels beneath the city of Ur, we sank a little shaft, not more than five feet [1.5 m] square at the outset, into the underlying soil and went down through the mixed rubbish that is characteristic of old inhabited sites—a mixture of decomposed mud brick, ashes and broken pottery, very much like that in which the graves had been dug. This went on for about three feet [0.9 m] and then suddenly, it all stopped:

An 18th-century view of the flood.

bad, and the pattern of the late 15th and early 16th centuries was no longer any guide to what to expect next.

Of course wine harvest alone cannot tell the complete story. But in that same half century, the glaciers of the mountains of Switzerland, Savoy and the Tyrol all expanded, pushing deeper into the mountain valleys. The onset of this sudden surge of cold, ushering in the worst century of the Little Ice Age in northeast Europe, is marked also in the pattern of tree rings and even in the subtle changes in chemical composition of snow being laid down in the glaciers of frozen Greenland. This was the period of the great 'Frost Fairs' on the River Thames at London, of conditions so severe in Scotland that King James VI, by then also King James I of England, used his authority in 1612 to establish a settlement of Scottish subjects in Ulster, an act that has its repercussions still in the troubles of Northern Ireland.

Nor did James's act do the Scots much good, for they continued to suffer through the 17th century. Between 1693 and 1700 there were seven harvest failures in eight years and death by starvation on a scale to

---

there were no more potsherds, no ashes, only clean water-laid mud, and the Arab workman at the bottom of the shaft told me that he had reached virgin soil; there was nothing more to be found, and he had better go elsewhere. I told the man to get back and go on digging. . . . Most unwillingly he did so, again turning up nothing but clean soil that yielded no sign of human activity; he dug through eight feet [2.4 m] of it in all and then, suddenly, there appeared flint implements and fragments of painted al 'Ubaid pottery vessels. I brought up two of my staff and, after pointing out the facts, asked for their explanation. They did not know what to say. My wife came along and looked and was asked the same question, and she turned away remarking casually, "Well, of course, it's the Flood." That was the right answer.'

An aerial shot of Ur in the 1930s, soon after the discovery that it had endured a catastrophic flood in the fourth millenium BC.

compare with anything occurring today in the Sahel. While other political factors undoubtedly played a part, there is no doubt that the desperate state to which Scotland was reduced by this century of vicious weather was one reason for the Union with England in 1707. Even in France and Italy the population was falling during this period, and Professor Hubert Lamb of the University of East Anglia has estimated that global population was falling in spite of a few pockets, such as Turkey and parts of Russia, that were benefiting from the climatic shift.

Cold summers and their effects on crops were far more important for human survival than icy winters, although the records of these make for more dramatic reading. And summer variability, rather than more winters like 1978, is the chief problem now facing the world's farmers once again. No one can say with absolute certainty which way the climate will shift next. But Professor Lamb has stressed that by the standards of the past millennium the early part of the 20th century brought the most unusual 50-year run of mild, predictable weather of any half century. Since the 1950s the temperature of the world has swung back sharply from these freak conditions, and all the signs are that things are going back to what has been normal in recent centuries— something much more like the Little Ice Age than like the mid-20th century. The causes of these changes will be discussed in the next chapter. But first a brief recap of just what a return to cooler and, most significantly, more *variable* weather, with

'WHEN ALL MANKIND WAS TURNED TO CLAY'

Besides the Biblical story of Noah, the best-known account of the Flood is found in the Babylonian *Epic of Gilgamesh*. This poem, describing Gilgamesh's search for immortality, dates back to about 2000 BC. In it, an old man, Ut-Napishtim, describes how he survived the Flood. This section of the epic remains one of the most powerfully evocative descriptions of the hurricane-force winds, the storm-surge and the torrential rain which flooded an area of about 400 square miles (1036 sq km) in the Tigris-Euphrates Valley. The parallels with the story of Noah, which is based on sources no older than the 8th century BC, are clear. In this extract, Ut-Napishtim has built the ark and shepherded in his family and flocks. He awaits the Flood, instigated by the goddess Ishtar:

'The time was fulfilled, the evening came, the rider of the storm sent down the rain. I looked out at the weather and it was terrible, so I too boarded the boat and battened her down. All was now complete, the battening and the caulking; so I handed the tiller to Puzur-Amurri the steersman, with the navigation and the care of the whole boat.

'With the first light of dawn a black cloud came from the horizon; it thundered within where Adad, lord of the storm was riding. In front over hill and plain Shullat and Hanish, heralds of the storm, led on. Then the gods of the abyss rose up; Nergal pulled out the dams of the nether waters, Ninurta the war-lord threw down the dykes, and the seven judges of hell, the Annunaki, raised their torches, lighting the land with their livid flame. A stupor of despair went up to heaven when the god of the storm turned daylight to darkness, when he smashed the land like a cup. One whole day the tempest raged, gathering fury as it went. It poured over the people like the tides of battle; a man could not see his brother nor the people be seen from heaven. Even the gods were terrified at the flood, they fled to the highest heaven, the firmament of Anu; they crouched against the walls, cowering like curs. Then Ishtar the sweet-voiced Queen of Heaven cried out like a woman in travail: "Alas the days of old are turned to dust because I commanded evil; why did I command this evil in the council of all the gods? I commanded wars to destroy the people, but are they not my people, for I brought them forth? Now like the spawn of fish they float in the ocean." The great gods of heaven and of hell wept, they covered their mouths.

For six days and six nights the winds blew, torrent and tempest and flood overwhelmed the world, tempest and flood raged together like warring hosts. When the seventh day dawned the storm from the south subsided, the sea grew calm, the flood was stilled; I looked at the face of the world and there was silence. All mankind was turned to clay.'

more extremes of all kinds, will mean.

Dr Martin Parry of the University of Birmingham, England, has made a particular study of the effect of extreme weather events in recent centuries on agriculture and society. His story makes grim reading. Taking just a few of the weather-induced crises recorded since the beginning of the Little Ice Age, in the years 1315–16 after a run of poor harvests, came a disastrous sequence of seasons. A wet, cold spring in 1315 was followed by great rains in the summer in Europe, so that the grain was washed away and lost by August; a further wet summer and widespread flooding the following year meant that yields of wheat on some English estates averaged 40 percent below the normal levels of the half century (1300 to 1350) for two years running, while the wet encouraged the spread of disease among cattle. The combined loss of crops and livestock brought the worst crisis in England since the Norman invasion of 1066, with widespread famine in Scotland.

In the years preceding the worst century of the Little Ice Age—conditions perhaps pointing most closely to what we can expect in the decades ahead—the 1590s brought a run of cool summers and famine across Europe. This time, a vicious winter in 1555 contributed to the hardship of the agricultural population and set the scene for three decades of poor summers and declining food reserves which built up to the crisis decade. Again Scotland suffered famine; laws restricting grain exports and the eating of meat came in to force; in Norway the grass died and there was widespread starvation; and into the 17th century a pattern of alternating extremes of weather swept Europe. Very harsh, cold winters and wet, stormy summers were followed by wet winters and hot summers, until the farmers hardly knew what to expect. A wet summer and autumn in 1648, for example, delayed autumn sowing of crops which failed to develop rapidly in the ensuing poor weather and brought a very late harvest in 1649 as well as dramatic rises in the price of staples such as oats.

From 1692 onwards came another terrible decade centered on the 'seven ill years' from 1692–99, which led to the abandonment of hill farms and marginal land in Scotland, a contributory factor in the depopulation of the Highlands. In Finland it is estimated as much as half the population died in the famine of 1696–97, while south, in France, the struggle against the weather hovered for a long time on the edge of a similar disaster.

Let us consider a few more isolated extremes: in 1782 late spring frosts and a cold summer left farmers in the Highlands of Scotland still harvesting the oat crop after Christmas in the snow; in 1816, with Europe in the aftermath of the Napoleonic wars, another cold summer (undoubtedly related to the explosion of a great volcano in the Far East in April 1815, throwing dust high into the stratosphere) more than doubled the price of oats in England, while in France the wine harvests were the latest in recorded history.

By this time we begin to have reliable reports of conditions in America, where New Englanders felt the coldest weather in June anyone could remember, and the corn and vegetable crop failed across the northeastern US.

From then on, by and large, conditions began to improve, but at the end of the 19th century came another sharp burst of cold and extremes. From 1879–81 liver-fluke disease, spread by damp summers, killed ten percent of sheep in Britain; from 1869–94, 100,000 cattle died of pleuropneumonia. This was already a time of agricultural depression and reduced prices; with adverse climate too, there was a widespread trend away from farming at moorland edges, with large areas going over to rough grass which in many places remains moorland to this day, in spite of the better weather of the mid-20th century.

In the 1960s and 1970s signs of another return of this kind of problem have again appeared. The winter of 1962–63 was the coldest in Europe for many years, with the heaviest snowfall in England for a hundred years. In Japan the winter of 1967–68 was unusually cold, yet in 1968–69 the winter was remarkably mild; in the 1970s England experienced a run of mild winters broken by weather as bad as 1962–63 in 1977–78: a record-breaking wet summer in 1977, and a record-breaking drought in 1976. The US, too, suffered both droughts and floods, along with the two 'once in a century' winters of 1976–77 and 1977–78. Indeed all the signs are that 19th-century weather is back, the prelude to a return to the Little Ice Age. But why? What causes these ups and downs of weather?

THE PEA-SOUPERS OF LONDON

For a century or more, London's fogs were legendary. Countless tales of crime and horror depend for their impact on the sinister blankets of gray and yellow. Only in the 1950s was it widely appreciated that such 'pea-soupers' were both deadly and unnecessary. As in Los Angeles and other large industrial centers, London's atmosphere trapped both fog and industrial pollutants to make smog, a lethal combination of smoke and fog. For decades, the murk was accepted as 'normal.' Then, in December 1952, London suffered one of the worst air pollution disasters ever. Shipping on the Thames came to a standstill. Firemen guided their vehicles by torchlight. The month's death-rate in Greater London rose by 3500, mostly elderly people with chronic bronchitis whose tattered lungs could not cope with the extra stress of filtering oxygen from the soupy atmosphere. Such a disaster could not be allowed to recur. Four years later, the Clean Air Act enforced the adoption of smokeless fuels and emission controls. Since then, smogs have all but vanished. Between 1956 and 1972 the density of smoke particles in the air dropped by 80 percent. London's air is cleaner now than it has been for 150 years.

Smog in Cannon Street.

Smog spreads in over Tower Bridge, 1937.

A London Transport Official holds a flare to guide a bus through the 1952 smog.

A flare marks a crossroads during the smog of December 1924.

A policeman on point duty wears a smog-mask to filter out the worst effects of pollution.

Mammoths migrate along the leading edge of an Ice Age glacier in Northern Europe some 15,000 years ago.

5: THE BROAD VIEW

Behind the short-term climatic changes indicated by historical evidence lie long-term patterns, with rhythms of hundreds of thousands of years. The evidence for the existence of these lies in the rocks of the Earth, in the changing pattern of the Earth's orbit and in the history of life on Earth.

A broad view of climatic change covers a wide sweep of time—hundreds of millions of years—and a vast sweep of space, across at least the 93 million miles (149 million km) to the Sun, and according to some ideas out across the immense reaches of space between the stars.

Geologists can track the history of ancient glaciations from the scars left in old rocks by the passage of glaciers. This information tells us that, on this longest of timescales, we are living in an Ice Age today, since the occurrence of *any* polar ice is a rare event in the long history of the Earth. It may be a warm bit of an Ice Age—an interglacial— but an Ice Age it is nonetheless. Ice Ages by this definition last for a few million years at a time, with several ebbs and flows of the great ice sheets during each Ice Age. Geologists find traces of other Ice Ages about 300, 450, 650, 900 and 1250 million years ago, and one school of thought suggests that the sudden appearance on Earth of creatures with shells 600 million years ago was a direct response to the cold of that time.

The unravelling of the saga of long-term climatic changes is complicated by the fact that, on this timescale, continents shift about the globe. It is little use knowing that the rocks of what is now Britain, say, were covered with ice 650 million years ago if we do not know where on the surface of the globe 'Britain' was then!

Continental drift has an additional significance for our theme. It now seems very likely that the movements of continents themselves play a part in the production of Ice Age conditions. Ice caps form more easily on land than on ocean, because snow can settle on land and build up into ice layers; and a small polar ocean surrounded by land masses can be cut off from the warming currents of the oceans near the equator and cool so much that a frozen crust of sea ice can form on top. These are just the conditions we have on Earth today— an almost land-locked polar sea in the north and a continent sitting squarely over the pole in the south (Antarctica). But this is very far from being a common condition on Earth, and for most of the Earth's five thousand million years the polar regions must have been much warmer, with polar seas bathed by currents from the equatorial oceans and no ice forming even at very high latitudes.

Unfortunately this neat concept cannot explain all the subtleties of the coming and going of ice sheets, and it cannot even explain why there seems to be a very rough 200- to 250-million-year-long 'rhythm' in the spacing of the great Ice Ages mentioned above. Almost certainly something outside our planet altogether is producing an influence which molds the climate here below. Astronomers are never afraid to make grand speculations, and a whole flock of ideas has sprung up around the theme of an outside influence producing icy conditions on Earth.

One scientific theory is now accepted as a partial explanation of the ebb and flow of ice sheets over timescales of a few thousand to a few hundred thousand years. It represents a triumph of discovery that is worth recording in some detail. The idea goes back at least to the beginning of this century; it appeared in its classic form in the work of Yugoslav astronomer Milutin Milankovich in the 1930s, but only became established in the eyes of professional meteorologists in the 1970s. It is summed up most simply in a calculation by Professor B J Mason, the Director-General of the UK Meteorological Office.

The Milankovich Model, as it is still called, explains detailed changes in ice cover *within* a full Ice Age (including the warm interglacial we are now experiencing) in terms of changes in the orbit of the Earth and the orientation of our planet relative to the Sun. Three separate cyclic changes in the Earth's movements combine to produce the overall variations in the solar radiation falling on the Earth.

The longest is a cycle of between 90,000 and 100,000 years over which the orbit of the Earth around the Sun 'stretches' from more circular to more elliptical and back again.

Next, there is a cycle of some 40,000 years over which the tilt of the Earth's axis—the cause of the seasons—varies as the Earth 'nods' up and down relative to the Sun.

Finally, the combined pull of the Sun and Moon on the Earth causes our planet to wobble like a spinning top as it orbits around the Sun, with a rhythm 21,000 years long.

These effects combine over thousands of years to produce changes in the average amount of heat falling on any one point.

Professor Mason went further to calculate just how much 'extra' heat would be needed to melt ice at high latitudes to bring on an interglacial (such as today's) and just how much summer heat must be 'lost' to account for the advance of the ice nearly 100,000 years ago. A variety of pieces of evidence, such as the record of changing sea levels and the scratches left by glaciers in the rocks, tell geologists how much ice was

around in each millennium over the past 100,000 years, and the Milankovich Model tells how much heat was arriving from the Sun each season. When Mason put the two sets of figures together, the agreement was impressive.

Between 83,000 and 18,000 years ago, the 'deficiency' of northern summer heat (insolation) added up to a staggering 4.5×10^{25} calories; dividing this vast number by the

Temperature changes over the last 800,000 years Changes in the amount of heavy oxygen in marine fossils, which is proportional to the amount of ice, correlates well with the variations in the heat from the Sun (middle) – variations caused by perturbations in the Earth's orbit and spin (bottom).

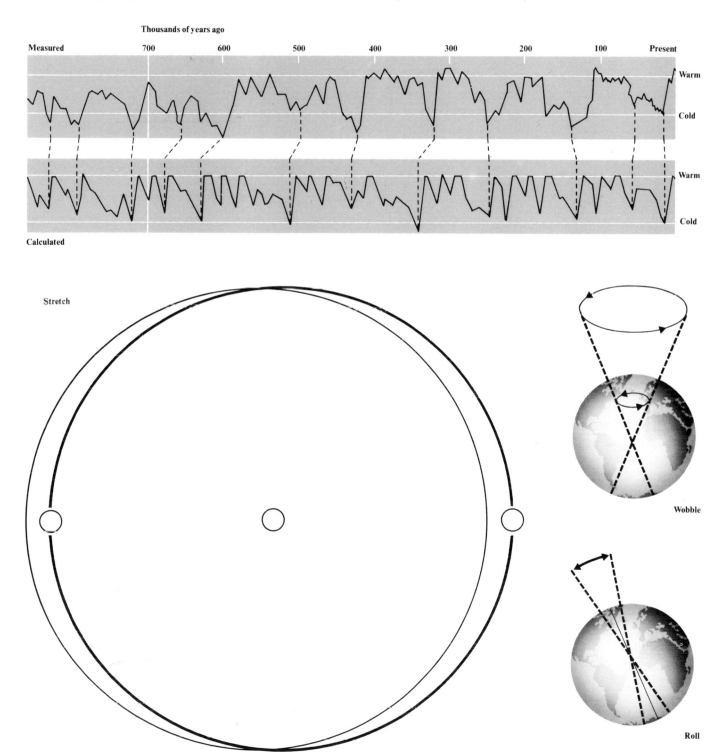

THE DEATH OF THE DINOSAURS: AN EXTENDED CATASTROPHE

One catastrophe that may indicate the onset of an Ice Age was the extinction of the dinosaurs 65 million years ago. The dinosaurs dominated life on land for 140 million years; yet they and their flying and swimming relatives—the pterosaurs and plesiosaurs—vanished in the course of just a few million years. Their disappearance remains largely unexplained, but it may have been related to climatic change. It is possible that a two-fold process worked against them. Continental drift, which ensures the formation of mountains along the colliding edges of continental plates and thus the creation of a wide variety of environments, may have slowed. If so, the mountains would have eroded, throwing formerly separated species into direct competition with each other. This could have combined with the onset of a cold spell that progressively locked up the waters of the Earth in the polar ice-caps. Sea-level would have dropped several hundred feet, exposing the continental shelves that bathed and warmed the continents and provided the environments in which the shallow-water marine reptiles thrived. By the end of the Cretaceous period, no land-based creatures of over about 22 lb (10 kg) survived (except for those whose niches remained intact, the crocodiles and turtles). The world was open for exploitation by those creatures that inhabited small-scale environments, the tiny, shrew-like mammals and the birds.

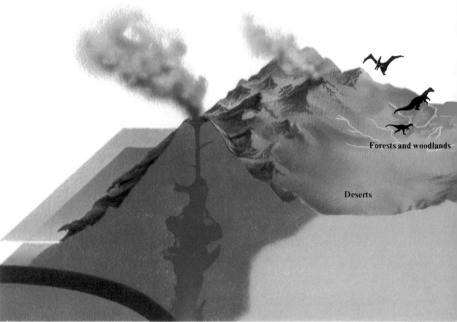

Subduction zone   Leading edge of continental plate: new mountains

Forests and woodlands

Deserts

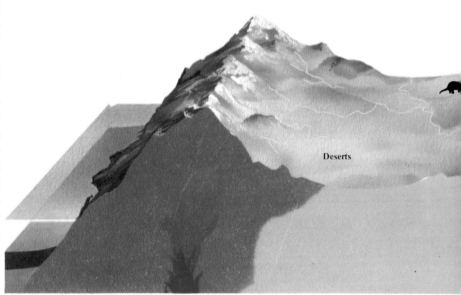

Deserts

Eroding mountains

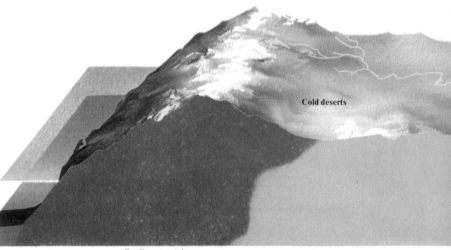

Cold deserts

Eroding mountains

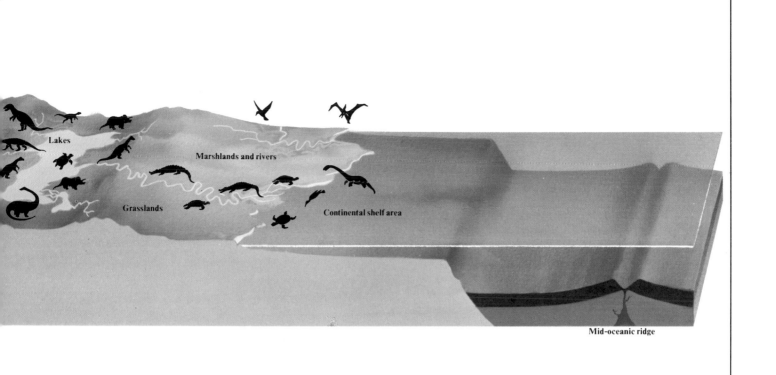

Mid-oceanic ridge

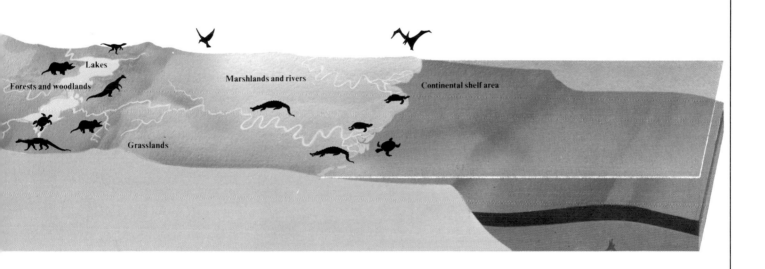

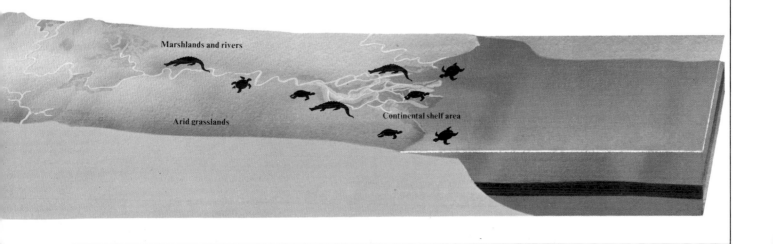

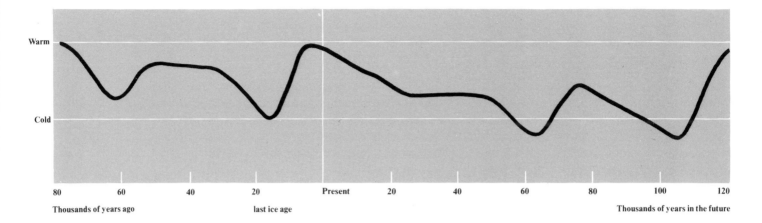

Warm

Cold

| 80 | 60 | 40 | 20 | Present | 20 | 40 | 60 | 80 | 100 | 120 |

Thousands of years ago　　　　　　　**last ice age**　　　　　　　**Thousands of years in the future**

If the rhythm of the past is extended into the future, it can be seen that we are heading into another Ice Age. We are, at present, about half-way through an interglacial period. On this scale, the warm spell over the first decades of this century was an aberration. The preceding Little Ice Age (*c*.1500–1850) provides a better indication of what is to come over the next few thousand years.

equally vast weight of the ice sheets which built up in the northern hemisphere at that time, Mason arrived at a more everyday figure—a 1000-calories deficiency for every gram of ice formed. When a gram of water vapor is cooled all the way down to a gram of ice, the amount of heat loss involved in the change is 677 calories. The Milankovich effect is more than enough (but only just) to account for the great freeze from 83,000 to 18,000 years ago.

What happens when the ice melts? Not quite so much 'extra' summer insolation is needed, because the ice only has to melt to water and run off into the sea; it does not have to be evaporated all the way back into vapor from its frozen state. From 18,000 years ago to the present, 4.2×10^{24} 'extra' calories were available from the changes of the Milankovich cycles; and the amount of heat needed to melt the ice that geologists know was melting over that time turns out to be 3.2×10^{24} calories. Again, the Milankovich effect is just a little bit bigger than the minimum needed to do the job. The 'coincidence' of the two figures suggests a cause-and-effect relationship; a 'coincidence' which stretches across 24 powers of ten with such accuracy cannot be anything else.

The model does also give us a long range forecast—the present interglacial is just about over and we are heading back into a period of colder northern summers and southern winters, with a new full Ice Age looming up no more than a few thousand years ahead.

Another theory relates Ice Age cycles to the time it takes our whole Solar System to orbit once about the center of our Milky Way Galaxy. This time—a kind of galactic

'year'—is also about a couple of hundred million years, and several variations on a theme have been produced to explain the coincidence of this timescale and the spacing of Ice Ages. The best of these ideas, although it is still far from being proven, is that at more or less regular intervals the Sun and Solar System plunge into dusty clouds of interstellar material, like those which can be seen edging the bright spiral arms of a typical galaxy. Dusty interstellar material might literally block out the Sun's heat for a few million years, causing an Ice Age, or more likely the effect of dust falling onto the Sun might upset its natural balance so much so that it temporarily goes 'off the boil,' producing a sequence of surface temperature changes that change the climatic conditions on Earth.

This second variation has also been invoked by some astronomers without the need for a dust cloud, since they argue that the nuclear fusion which powers our Sun can from time to time build up a kind of nuclear 'ash' inside, damping down the nuclear fires until a hiccup in the solar interior restores things to normal.

Either way the theories remain grand speculation, and certainly not of any great significance for mankind on a timescale of a mere few thousand years, let alone next week or next year. Even the fluctuations in temperature and ice cover of the globe over the past two million years are rather beyond the scope of our look at the way weather force affects our lives here and now, although the erratic ups and downs of the curve do serve as a reminder that our idea of what is 'normal' is very much colored by experience that is very limited.

Apart from changes in the influence of the Sun itself, the Earth is also constantly

CAN METEORS TRIGGER ICE AGES ?

One of the more way-out explanations of the onset of ice ages is that a giant meteorite may occasionally strike the Earth from space, landing in an ocean. Paradoxically, although great meteorites can produce more damage than a nuclear bomb when they hit on land, an ocean strike may produce much greater repercussions world-wide. Such a giant mass of rock would give up all its energy of motion (kinetic energy) in the form of heat. Racing through the atmosphere almost unaffected, the impacting meteorite would vaporize a hole right through the ocean to the sea-floor, where it would strike with the force of many nuclear bombs, blasting a crater which could rip away the thin crust of rock of the sea-bed, allowing molten rock (magma) from the layers below to flood into the crater. As the waters of the ocean rushed in, they would vaporize explosively into steam, creating a pall of clouds which would blanket the world before the waters could quench the fires of the crater. As the seas subsided back towards normality, a salt rain would fall around the world, and temperatures would fall dramatically as the cloud cover blocked out the heat from the Sun, so that the rain would turn to snow at high latitudes.

Enough snow lying at high latitudes could keep the Earth cool even when the cloud cover began to break up months later, since the shiny white snowfields would reflect away as much solar heat as the clouds had. A new Ice Age would have begun, in the most catastrophic way imaginable.

Most climatologists dismiss this idea as so improbable that it can be ruled out of serious considerations—and yet, full Ice Ages only begin every two or three hundred million years, so that *whatever* it is that triggers them off must indeed be a rare and improbable event, or sequence of events. And it seems highly likely that the Earth has been struck by massive chunks of rock a number of times in the past. It has been suggested that naturally circular coastlines—like the bulge of West Africa or the coast of China—could be the result of ancient strikes of the size that caused large lunar craters. And there are other, smaller bays, like the Nastapoka curve in Hudson's Bay, that are even more suggestive of the edge of craters.

To get some idea of the scale of such an event, we can use the calculations presented by J E Enever in the March 1966 issue of the science fiction magazine *Analog*—for a four-cubic-mile (16 cubic km) meteor, rather smaller than many known asteroids, colliding with the Earth at a velocity of 30 miles (50 km) a second (modest in terms of meteorite impact velocities). The energy released would be six million times as great as that from the explosion of Krakatoa in 1883. We know that Krakatoa produced a measurable effect on global climate; what would the effect of that change multiplied six million times look like? Here we certainly edge into the realms of science fiction: a tidal wave hundreds of feet high, rain and snow for years, a long-term cooling—and the rapid arrival of another Ice Age.

Large curves in the Earth's land masses – like the bulge of China and the inlet of Hudson Bay shown below – have suggested to some Earth scientists the possibility that the Earth has been struck by large meteorites in the past. Such impacts would probably bring world-wide climatic changes.

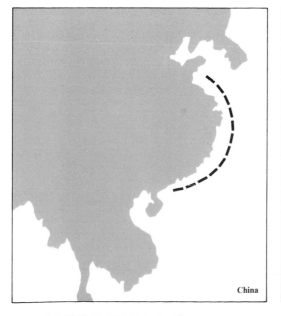

China

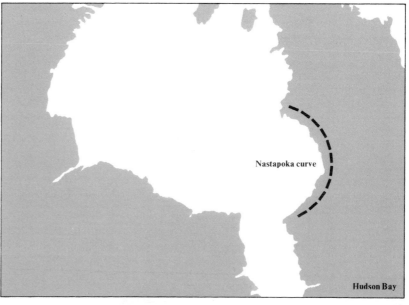

Nastapoka curve

Hudson Bay

A fossilized tree in
Glasgow – evidence of a
former tropical climate.

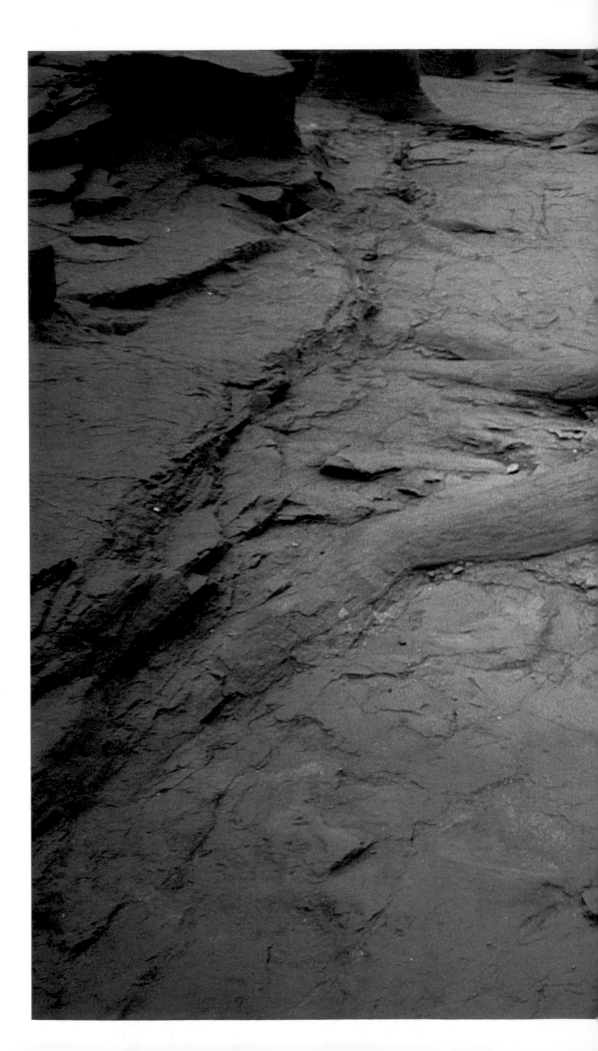

subjected to a flood of particles from space, the so-called 'cosmic rays.' Some of these come from the Sun, blasted out when the Sun flares into activity, as it does from time to time. Others come from beyond the Solar System, the products of stellar explosions far away in space and long ago in time. All of these are affected by the magnetic fields of the Sun and the Earth, sometimes penetrating strongly into the Earth's atmosphere, especially near the poles where the magnetic field has 'holes,' sometimes scarcely penetrating at all.

Here, too, is a way for extraterrestrial influences to affect the atmosphere of our planet, and especially the critical ozone layer of the stratosphere, above about 12.5 miles (20 km) altitude, which plays a key role as the 'lid' on the troposphere, or weather layer, in which we live below.

Ozone is a three-atom molecule of oxygen produced by the interaction of sunlight with the two-atom molecules of oxygen that are common in the atmosphere, the kind that we breathe. These interactions warm up the stratosphere so that a layer of relatively warm air sits on top of the troposphere ('relatively' is the key word—at these altitudes 32°F [0°C], freezing point for water, is 'warm'!). This stops convection rising above 12.5 miles (20 km) altitude, and as we saw in Chapter 2 convection is a key part of the weather machine. Any great change in ozone—more *or* less—can directly influence the circulation of the atmosphere in the troposphere below, and strong bursts of cosmic ray particles from space could act to break up ozone, weakening the influence of the stratosphere and upsetting the weather systems below. What the effects would be we can only guess—and, inevitably, some guesses are that this effect too could be a trigger for Ice Ages. Once again, though, there is no reason to believe that anything like this is going to happen in the next few years, since the Earth's magnetic field seems well able to withstand cosmic ray particles at present.

We are on stranger ground when we turn to the ways geological events affect climate and weather. A key factor seems to be the influence of dust from volcanoes. Volcanic dust spread high enough in the atmosphere cools the Earth by reflecting back into space heat from the Sun that would otherwise reach the ground.

The dust literally acts as a sunshield. Great volcanic eruptions have been clearly linked with cool decades on Earth during the past few centuries, chiefly through the work of British climatologist Professor H H Lamb. The implications of this connection for human society have been spelled out by an American climatologist, Professor Reid Bryson, notably in his book (with Thomas Murray) *Climates of Hunger*.

The year 1816 was one of the coldest on record, we already know. And it came just after a great eruption in Indonesia in the year 1815. The explosion of Krakatoa in 1883 brought measured temperatures around the globe down by a fraction of a degree for a decade, with an estimated 13 cubic miles (50 cu km) of dust blown to great altitudes and over great distances, so that spectacular sunsets were seen around the world for months after the eruption.

It is rare for just one volcano to have such a huge effect, but many smaller volcanoes active together have a comparable impact. The middle part of the present century was remarkably free from volcanic activity around the globe although there were some eruptions, and these were also decades of relatively mild, stable weather. Is this mere coincidence? In the middle of the 1970s volcanic activity seemed to be picking up again, releasing more dust into the atmosphere. Does this herald a rapid cooling and retreat into more extreme patterns of weather? Climatologists such as Professor Bryson argue that it does, and he describes how the effect operates:

'Dust in the atmosphere tends to cool the high latitudes more than it does the tropical regions, no matter where it enters the atmosphere. Some dust is carried poleward, over a period of weeks and months, by the high-altitude flow of air from the tropics. More important, even if dust were distributed evenly throughout the atmosphere, the poleward regions would be more shaded than the tropics. Sunlight takes a nearly vertical path through the atmosphere in the tropics, but away from them comes in at an angle, and therefore has a longer path through the atmosphere. If the atmosphere is dusty, the sunlight has a longer path through the dust—and is diminished all along the way.'

While accepting that other factors also

affect the changing climate. Professor Lamb has noted that volcanic dust seems to have played a part in all of the very worst summers in Britain, North America and Japan of the 17th to the 20th centuries, and says that there is a clear tendency for cold winters in Europe to follow volcanic eruptions, even at low latitudes, that produce global dust veils. This is precisely in line with Bryson's explanation quoted above.

Looking back into the record of past climates, geologists can contribute to the picture by their analyses of layers of volcanic ash found in different strata around the world. Epochs of increased volcanic activity can be recognized in this way—decades, centuries or even millennia when the entire Earth was convulsed by a series of events which produced a great outpouring of volcanic dust. These may have been events tied in with the broad sweep of geological processes, like collisions between continents. Or they may have been times when more subtle factors, outside influences (perhaps even the impact of a giant meteorite) or forces as yet unknown caused the upsurge in global volcanism. Whatever the cause, though, the evidence remains in the rocks. And the rocks show a very close correlation between increases in global volcanic activity and cold epochs with advancing ice sheets at high latitudes.

New Zealander Dr J M Bray has produced a study going back just over 40,000 years, covering the last half of the latest icy epoch, which shows that many large-scale eruptions occurred just before the advance of the ice sheets. In the past 17,200 years in particular, there have been 18 phases of widespread global activity and related advances of the ice, with the delay between volcanic outbursts and ice advance averaging between 100 and 300 years. This study in no way undermines the Milankovich Model, but rather shows why ice should advance in one particular century of a 40,000-year cycle rather than in another century. In addition sometimes the ice advances without volcanic dust giving an extra push, and sometimes the volcanoes erupt without a resulting surge of the glaciers—further evidence that forces other than volcanoes are at play in molding the climate.

Some geologists have even argued that, rather than volcanic activity triggering ice advance, it is the weight of the ice spreading over the land that triggers off regions of volcanic instability, squeezing magma out from below the Earth's crust like tooth-

A house in Heimaey, an island a few miles off southern Iceland, almost invisible under a mountain of ash and lava after an eruption in January 1973 – a dramatic reminder of the amount of dust that even a minor eruption can throw into the atmosphere.

REMINDERS OF AN AGE OF ICE

That the northern parts of Europe and America were once covered by huge sheets of ice is historically a relatively new idea. In 1837 a young Swiss naturalist, Louis Agassiz, pointed out that across northern Europe there were many rocks that seemed to have been polished by ice and strange mounds of rock and gravel that seemed to mark the limits of glaciers. He suggested the only explanation was that ice really *had* been responsible.

His theory was accepted because it explained many other oddities about the geology of North America and northern Europe: stone-filled clays smeared over the landscapes, valleys carved into U-shapes as if by giant chisels, lakes of melt-water.

It is now known that there was not one Ice Age, but many—eight in the last 700,000 years. It is hard to date them, for one Ice Age erradicates the evidence of the previous one. The best evidence comes from the intact fossil records. These make it possible to provide an accurate profile of the last great advance, which began about 40,000 years ago. Gradually, many feet of ocean water were deposited at the poles.

Southern Alaska, almost all of Canada and the northern parts of the US disappeared under an ice sheet 1000–1500 yards thick. On the east coast, its terminal morraine is Long Island. In Europe the glaciers ended at a line running just north of London across to Berlin. The Mediterranean was dry and cold. Other ice-caps formed in the Alps and the Pyrenees. Only when the ice began to retreat 18,000 years ago did man begin to spread northwards.

The extent of the last great ice sheet 18,000 years ago.

□ Land ice

▨ Sea ice

A superb example of a
roche moutonné – a 'sheep-
shaped rock' – in Wales,
a rock rounded and polished
by the passage of a glacier
over it.

A bank of gravel in
Cumberland, dumped by
a glacier on its retreat
some 10,000 years ago.

A U-shaped valley in
Wales, gouged out by ice.

paste squeezed from a tube. Dr Bray's study seems to refute that argument, at least for the short term, with volcanic outbursts definitely occurring *before* the glaciers advanced. But it might still apply in the broader context of the great sweep of Ice Ages, and there is certainly no doubt that, one way or another, volcanic activity has been much higher during the past couple of million years—the great Ice Age—than during most of the past 20 million years. For the immediate future, however, the importance of the link between dust and climate lies not so much in the activity of volcanoes as in the activities of mankind — where Professor Bryson sounds a grim warning.

Here and now the problem is not so much one of dust from volcanoes, says Professor Bryson, as dust from factory chimneys, from wind blown soil, from engine exhausts

A man-made volcano? Pollution like this, reduplicated world-wide over many decades, may have the climatic impact of countless volcanic eruptions.

and from the fires of 'slash-and-burn' agriculture in the Third World. More than 500 million tons of dust now get into the atmosphere each year through these processes, and according to Bryson the amount that remains drifting high above the ground to obscure solar heat is about 15 million tons at present, equivalent to the burden from a moderate volcano. The effect of this burden is to cool the globe, especially at high latitudes, encouraging the development of an expanded circumpolar vortex with weaker circulation and hastening a return to the violently variable weather that had been common for a thousand years prior to the 20th century.

On the other hand, optimists may prefer to give equal weight to an opposite viewpoint, deriving from another aspect of human activity, the production of carbon dioxide from the burning of fossil fuels. The best evidence here is that in this case the effect is running against the cooling trend of nature. Carbon dioxide gas in the atmosphere acts as a blanket to warm the globe, trapping heat near the ground by the so-called 'greenhouse effect.' So man's activities here may be helping to warm the Earth and stave off a rapid decline into what might otherwise be a new trough of the Little Ice Age.

Scientists are still arguing about just how big this effect might be and whether or not it might cancel out Bryson's human volcano effect. To resolve the issue, we must ask how much fossil fuel can we burn before a long-lasting climate shift becomes established? And it is also worth asking: will such damage be necessarily bad?

Since the late 19th century, the concentration of carbon dioxide in the air has increased from about 290 parts per million (ppm) to about 330 ppm, a trend which is certainly significant and which coincides with the growth of industry world-wide. One study, by the International Institute of Applied Systems Analysis), has analyzed what could happen if carbon dioxide as a result of pollution triples (as it may do) by the mid-21st century.

The best rule of thumb at present (though not yet a concensus view) is that a doubling of carbon dioxide would result in a 2°F (1°C) rise in average temperatures, with more pronounced effects at high latitudes.

Such a shift would, by decreasing the temperature difference between poles and equator, shift climate and rainfall belts; but these models must still be taken with a large pinch of salt, as they do not include such important effects as changes in cloud cover. A warmer Earth, with increased evaporation from the oceans, ought to be a more cloudy place (with increased rainfall), and clouds tend to reflect heat from the Sun away before it reaches the ground, perhaps cancelling out part of the warming induced by carbon dioxide.

The study foresees world demands for energy levelling off early in the 21st century. It does not include significant use of any energy sources except coal, oil and gas. (Coal is the only long-term fossil fuel, with reserves that could last centuries compared with just decades for oil and gas.) In such a scenario, by the end of the next century, the world will be 6°F (3°C) hotter. The temperature change starts to dominate over any natural trends in about 50 years time, when it reaches a magnitude of 2°F (1°C). But it would be far too late to wait until then to attempt to restore the natural balance, as it takes decades to change the pattern of primary energy use, or indeed to achieve wide-spread use of 'pollution' controls on carbon dioxide.

In some ways, the projections are a 'worst possible' case. With any significant use of solar, wave or nuclear power, or any effective controls on the amount of carbon dioxide released, or any effective means of disposing of the gas other than release to the atmosphere, the figures for carbon dioxide in the atmosphere and the resulting change in global temperature will be less. What the projections tell us is that one or more of these options must be taken up soon— unless there is some good reason to accept that the consequence of a rise in global temperatures of 6°F (3°C) or more is something that our grandchildren will be happy to live with.

It would be mischievous to suggest, given the present state of the art in climate studies, that a significantly warmer Earth might be a better place to live in, and that we therefore should not worry about the likely carbon-dioxide-induced warming of the 21st century. But it is just as mischievous to assume, as so many people do, that a warmer Earth must be a worse place to live and therefore that panic measures are necessary to preserve the *status quo*. Perhaps there *is* some reason to believe that a slight warming might be welcome, given the perspective of the past thousand years or so.

Professor Will Kellogg, of the US National Center for Atmospheric Research, has tried to sketch out what a 40°F (20°C) rise might mean for agriculture and human society by comparison with the previous warm epoch, the so-called Climatic Optimum of 4000 to 8000 years ago.

This model shows us a warm Earth with conditions more favorable for agriculture in North Africa, Europe wetter, Scandinavia drier, and a belt of grasslands across North America. Such a warm Earth would be by no means a less desirable place in which to live, and the rainfall patterns in particular seem to be more favorable to agricultural production globally than those of today. At the same time, the increased growing season produced by a warmer climate would also help agriculture.

The argument in favor of the *status quo*, is that we do manage (just) to cope with the vagaries of the present climate, and any change is going to require a painful period of adjustment in farming practices and food trade. But the possibility of having a climate more suitable for feeding a large population should also be taken into account when the 'danger' of an imminent carbon-dioxide-induced global warming is being discussed.

One thing is certain—the temperature changes that have taken place in the 20th century *so far*, both the initial warming and the cooling we are now experiencing, cannot be explained solely in terms of the influence of mankind, and the day when our own pollution outweighs the effects of natural forces still lies in the future— although perhaps no further away than the end of this century. For the next 20 years, we have to continue to cope with the forces of nature and their natural trends, those trends which unmistakably point us into another spell of violent weather and extreme variations from place to place and from season to season. As Bryson says, 'More important than the cooling itself is the resulting change in the westerlies to patterns that are more expanded and more looping.' We can expect 'drought in the monsoon lands and elsewhere, shorter growing seasons in the world's main food-producing areas, and more highly variable weather.' And where does this leave us, in a world where, we are told, starvation is already rife?

BLANKETS OF ASH AND DUST

One factor among the many that contribute to change the world's climate over the centuries may be the amount of dust thrown up by volcanoes. For instance, the great eruption of Krakatoa in 1883——the most massive volcanic explosion in recent times—reduced the intensity of the Sun's heat world-wide by an estimated 20–30 percent. Individually, most 'average' volcanoes, like Vesuvius (which has erupted many times since it buried Pompei in AD 79) and Surtsey, add infinitesimally to the 'dust veil index.' When Monte Pelée in Martinique exploded in 1902—with effects that are recorded in this picture feature—it probably dimmed the incoming energy from the Sun by only 2–3 percent.

It would take a truly monumental series of world-wide eruptions to bring on an Ice Age, and the effect of even the most massive historical volcanoes has probably been to create only a minor hiccup in a current trend. But even that could be enough to damage harvests world-wide for a year or two.

The birth of Surtsey, a volcanic island off Iceland, in 1963.

The 1845 eruption of Vesuvius, which has exploded into life several times in recorded history.

A cauliflower cloud of
dust over Vesuvius in 1944
shows how an eruption
can throw tens of thousands
of tons of volcanic material
many miles into the upper
atmosphere, where it forms
a world-wide filter for the
Sun's rays.

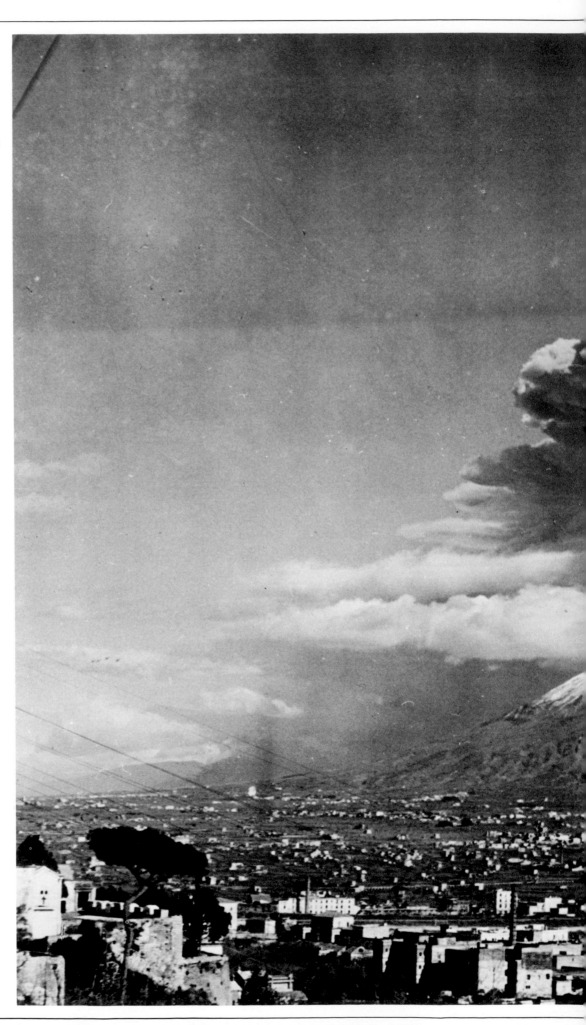

St Pierre in ruins, as if hit by an atomic bomb.

One of the several *nuées ardentes* or 'glowing clouds' released by Mont Pelée in 1902. In one such explosion on 8 May super-heated gases and

The lava plug that sealed the volcano after the 1902 eruption.

incandescent particles exploded downhill at 180 mph (290 kph) and annihilated the town of St Pierre and its 30,000 inhabitants within three minutes.

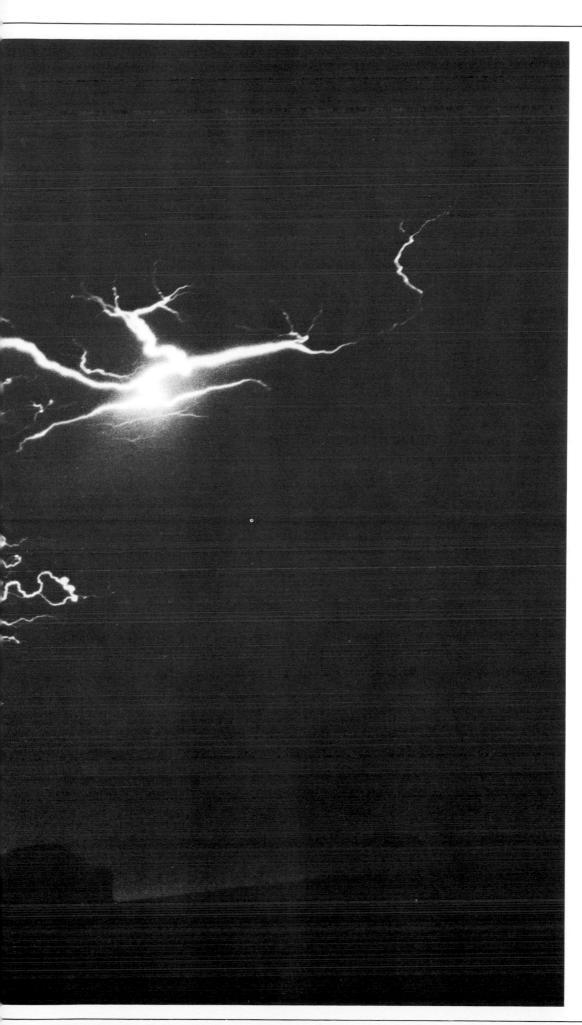

Lightning flickers through the pall of volcanic dust thrown up by the Surtsey eruption.

A Mauritanian farmer
slakes his thirst while
seeding an arid, sandy field
that may be reverting
permanently to desert.

6:CLIMATE AND FOOD

In underdeveloped nations, many millions live in a world under the permanent threat of ecological catastrophe. In the Indian sub-continent, in West Africa, in South America, floods or droughts bring starvation. International action can mitigate the worst effects of climatic disasters, but with a climate possibly changing for the worse and a steadily rising world population, the international response will have to be far more radical.

We have seen that the Earth is now experiencing a detrimental climatic shift—detrimental in terms of impact on global agriculture—and that nothing man can do, by accident or design, is going to change the natural trend before the end of this century. During the 1970s we have all read in our papers and been told on TV and the radio that the world is rapidly becoming overpopulated, and that even without any nudge from the weather, mass starvation is just around the corner. 'Zero growth' has become a fashionable concept.

But what good is zero growth if conditions for life on Earth get harsher? The traditionally precarious interrelationship between climate and food is at a turning point. We could, in theory, feed our world, if we had a mind to. We could, in theory, overcome the worst effects of a few bad years. Let us start our analysis of this somewhat unfashionable view by asking: Why do people *really* starve? And what are the *real* figures for the maximum sustainable—or desirable—human population of our planet?

Certainly people are starving today—millions of people. We know about this in more detail than ever before, owing to modern global communications. But when you look at the figures in detail it turns out that a smaller *proportion* of the world's population goes hungry today than ever before; and when one examines the other side of the coin, food production and agricultural potential, it becomes apparent that we could comfortably provide enough food for at least twice the present world population, with no dramatic changes in farming practice or food technology. New crops, better agriculture and so on could provide a bonus on top of this to support a much greater population still, if we really wanted to.

Yet the irony remains. People do starve today, and with virtually no reserves of food on a global scale we are balanced on a knife-edge where any harmful shift in climate can bring tragedy to whole regions of the globe as the case of the Sahel drought shows.

In Chapter 1 we saw how drought has wrecked the delicate agricultural balance of the regions along the southern fringe of

The effect of drought on one species, the buffalo, in one area, North Australia. The buffalo at left broke through the cracked surface of a swamp

in its search for water. Hundreds more had to be slaughtered (right).

the Sahara desert in the Sahel region of Africa. Armed now with an understanding of the climatic and weather forces at work in the region and world-wide, we can seek the root causes of this continuing drought, the drought that will not go away. The example of the Sahel shows just what can go wrong when mankind is too complacent, expecting things to continue in the old pattern, and expecting nature to be bountiful enough to make good the mistakes of mankind.

In the early 1970s the Sahel region made headlines, and the belt of drought could be seen as extending from the Sahel proper across through Ethiopia to northwest India. The partial break in the drought in 1974 pushed the disaster out of the news; the return of severe conditions in the past few years has received no more than minor attention on the inside pages of the newspapers. Yet the reality is as bad as ever and the prognostications more gloomy, in many respects, than before.

Dr Derek Winstanley, a British meteorologist now based in Canada, has made a long study of the droughts of this region and their links with the present global climatic shift. While the belt south of the Sahara is drying out, rainfall along North Africa's Mediterranean coast has been increasing—both effects associated with a southward push of northern hemisphere climatic zones, and expansion of the circumpolar vortex. The shift of the desert south is part of a natural global pattern— but one in which human activities are

In the early 1970s, Tsavo National Park, Kenya, was ravaged by drought. Here, two elephants search vainly for food and water.

hastening the process of desertification.

In the 1960s rainfall improved in this semi-desert region at the same time that well-intended aid programs from the richer countries of the developed world were providing many new wells to tap underground water supplies. Vaccination programs helped to reduce cattle disease and death, and the overall result was a boom decade of greatly increased human population, carried by the great increase in available water and the increasing herds of cattle. As soon as the rains declined from their unusual peak levels, the large herds began to take their toll of the now struggling pastureland. First dried out and then picked clean by the cattle, the semi-arid pasture quickly reverted to desert, pushing the nomadic herdsmen south into slightly less arid regions, where their herds combined with those of the people already living there to spread desertification faster and farther south. Eventually the cattle died too, but by then the damage had been done. The natural spread of desert southward with the fading rains had been hastened by the influence of man and his animals. And it is much easier to hasten desertification than to roll back the desert and reclaim what has been lost.

Even so, the warning signs were already present before the beginning of the massive expansion which at least doubled the extent of the disaster. As long ago as the 1930s there were signs that the climatic zones were beginning to be squeezed towards the equator, and only the simplest study of past records could have shown in the 1960s that the rains that were then common were simply too good to last. It is easy now— with all the advantages of hindsight—to see that a little planning to cope with the day the rains failed would have done more good than massive exploitation of the slender resources that were available.

The figures show that even when the rains 'returned' in 1974 and 1975 they reached only 90 percent of what used to be thought of as 'normal'—and that 90 percent is beginning to look increasingly like an unusual high peak by the new 'normal' standards. In 1976 rainfall dropped away again to 30 percent below the old normal, and through 1977 and 1978 the story was much the same.

Again, exactly in line with the expected influence of an expanded circumpolar vortex, the severity of the drought depends mainly on latitude. New studies reported by Dr Winstanley in 1978 show that in the semi-desert region around 18° North, rainfall was only 50 percent of the old normal for the period 1968–76, but with things less bad farther south. During the 16 years since they gained independence from the old colonial governments, the countries of the Sahel have, overall, suffered a decline in rainfall of 20 percent compared with the preceding 30 years—a cruel blow at the most critical time in the life of an emerging nation.

How far will things go before they get better? Dr Winstanley draws a parallel with the English drought of 1976, the worst heatwave for more than 200 years, and the severe winters, worst for at least a century, in the US and elsewhere in the late 1970s. Just as rainfall was abnormally high in Britain and Europe, on this longer perspec-

tive, during the 1950s and 1960s, so it was in the Sahel. Drier conditions, there as in the north, could in fact be more normal, argues Winstanley. And he makes the all-important link with political action, the link that is a vital part of the 'world food problem':

'In the early 1970s many governments of these countries were unwilling to seek international aid at an early stage of the drought, because they regarded the famines as something to be hushed up, an indication of the failure of their domestic policies. Will they be more willing to seek aid now, with the realization that natural global forces are contributing to their hardship? Or must the poorest inhabitants of those countries suffer once again while their leaders pretend that nothing is amiss?'

Climatic changes have entered the political arena world-wide with the realization that world population continues to rise while the climate deteriorates. The CIA released two reports in 1977 stressing this problem and drawing particular attention to the prospect of reduced crop yields in the Soviet Union in the decades ahead. If the USSR comes on to the world grain markets as a regular purchaser of 20 million tons of grain a year, then the whole structure of the world grain markets could be distorted. The United States, the world's main grain supplier, would benefit from this both commercially and politically, having a food 'lever' to use in other areas to pry concessions out of the USSR. But unless at least this much *extra* grain is being grown in the US, someone else will have to go without.

As things are today the people and nations that would inevitably suffer most will be the poorest—those who simply cannot afford to pay the same price for the available food that the USSR can: Will the Third World sit back and let this happen? The CIA sees a looming threat of mass migrations, political disturbances and retaliatory use of oil sanctions against the rich 'West' by Third World countries. With this extra burden on top of the many gloomy prognostications of reports such as the Club of Rome's notorious *Limits to Growth*, it might really seem that this time 'the end of the world is nigh.'

The truth, however, is less gloomy than the CIA or the prophets of doom—or

FAMINE IN ETHIOPIA

The tragedy of the Sahel famine (see pp. 150–157) were starkest in Ethiopia, which hid its starvation for as long as possible and neglected to feed the dying from its own resources. Not until October 1973, when more than 100,000 were already dead, did the Ethiopian government admit that up to 4000 were perishing every week. Relief workers were horrified to see scenes like those reproduced on this and the following pages.

Famine victims are brought to a relief camp by wheelbarrow.

Remains of a bullock on a once fertile plain.

A woman mourns her dead husband.

indeed the tragedy of the Sahel—suggest. It may not be easy, but even in a changing climate we can grow enough food for everyone—even our growing population—if we, as a global society, really want to make the effort.

Before we know how much food the world needs, we have to have some idea how much food each person needs. The pessimists—the 'Club of Rome' school—have used a rather high estimate of 2200 to 3000 calories per day, with 70 gm of protein (more than half of it animal protein); they also claim that 95 percent of all available land in Southeast Asia (to name one threatened area) is already used for agriculture to back their prognostications of imminent mass starvation. Yet since the early 1950s world food production has gone up on average by 2.8 percent a year, while population has been rising at two percent a year; and even the official estimates of the Food and Agriculture Organization (FAO) of the UN showed that in 1970 every person in the world could have had 2420 calories of food if the known marketed supplies had been evenly distributed. This figure, already in line with the high estimate of individual needs, takes no account of all the food grown and eaten by farmers and their families—or even in back gardens in countries like Britain and the US—without ever getting on to world food markets.

Those official UN figures for 1970 come out as the equivalent of 500 pounds of grain needed per person per year. On average during the 1970s about 1300 million tons of grain have reached markets each year—enough to feed the world's 4000 million people—and another 1000 million extra.

The truth is, then, that people do not starve because there is insufficient food in the world. The poor starve because they do not have enough money to compete in world food markets with the rich nations of North America and Europe, where people eat not only much more than they need but often much more than is good for them. We need to look at this dilemma, against a background of deteriorating climate, in two ways:

—First, by studying what happens when disastrous weather hits some part of the globe, the kind of situation that is becoming increasingly common as the 1970s give way to the 1980s.

—then we have to look at how the world really could feed everyone adequately, with a surplus of food built up in the good years to provide a buffer against famine in the lean years. It should be no surprise that one of the leading American climatologists, Dr Stephen Schneider, has summed this up as 'The Genesis Strategy' after the Biblical seven fat years and seven lean—the difference is that as things are now in our fat years we neglect to store anything up for the future.

There is no getting away from the dominant role played by North America in the world food markets today. By the mid-1970s the US and Canada stood almost alone as exporters of food grains in the world—some other countries or regions are nearly self-sufficient, and the rest depend on imports—imports from North America. The 90+ percent proportion of the world food market that is taken up by grains from the US and Canada is a bigger fraction than the proportion of the oil market supplied by the Middle East. So even internal (domestic) decisions about agriculture in the US and Canada are important for the hungry nations of the world today.

To many of the world's hungry, those decisions must seem baffling. How would one explain to a starving African farmer, whose crops have been destroyed by drought, that during the 1960s and early 1970s it was official US policy to pay some farmers *not* to grow grain but to leave their land idle in the so-called 'land bank'? The reason? Simply that US policy was to avoid producing so much grain that prices fell on the world market and so reduced the country's income. With the severe global weather problems in the early 1970s, demand for food rose; so did prices; and the land bank was put into profitable production again by 1973–74. But was the lesson learned? Far from it—a slight alleviation of the weather troubles a couple of years later, and in 1978 and 1979 the talk was once again of the need to avoid 'over-production' and to maintain prices—in other words, to stop growing grain on some of the land, let the prices rise again—and thus let poorer nations go hungry. Stephen Schneider has put the figures in perspective in his book *The Genesis Tragedy*. The 1974 World Food Conference called for ten million tons of grain to check famine in the world—an amount that represented less than five percent of the potential produce of US land deliberately kept idle through 1970–73. Schneider sums up the situation early in the last quarter of the 20th century: 'Dangerously depleted food reserves, low levels of fertilizer stock, high energy prices, and 80 million new mouths to feed yearly.'

Clearly someone should, in theory, hold food stocks against needs like those of 1974. But who? Individual governments, most importantly the US government, say that it is not their responsibility. Could the FAO or a new body under the umbrella of the UN take on the job? Perhaps—but then, who pays, and how does the UN force the US, say, to grow grain rather than leaving crop-land idle? As things stand we continue to stumble along from one crisis to another, a situation in which increased weather variability must inevitably bring famine to parts of the increasingly populous Third World at the same time that it reduces yields of harvests in North America, the world's breadbasket.

Just what *are* the effects of increasing weather variability on the food grain production of

MYTHS OF THE WORLD FOOD CRISIS

In their early concern not to underestimate world food requirements, the FAO assumed that an adequate diet for one person anywhere in the world would be that which was sufficient to keep a North American industrial worker fit and well. They therefore accepted a base figure of 3000 calories, including 90 gm of protein per day, a figure that has become established in studies of world food needs. Because some people get more food than others, however, some experts have taken this figure and *increased* it by a further 20 percent to allow for people who get less than average. The result was that when the base 'need' was simply multiplied by the population of a country—including babies and the aged—the FAO food requirement came out as much as four times more than the food that was actually being eaten and was maintaining a healthy population. In fact, even adult males need less food than an American industrial worker doing heavy labor in a cool climate.

During the 1960s, in addition to the concern about lack of total food, much was made of the so-called 'protein gap.' Relief agencies reported from the hungry regions of the world many severe cases of deficiency diseases, such as kwashiorkor and marasmas, identified with lack of protein. But again the concern turns out to have been misguided. More recently, it has been confirmed that when the body has insufficient basic food—calories in whatever form—then it begins to absorb its own protein, ie muscle (including heart muscle) simply to maintain life. Once the calorie intake can be increased sufficiently, with no additional protein food, then the body rebuilds its own muscle and the protein deficiency symptoms disappear.

These and similar studies have led to a steady reduction in the estimates of how much food each person needs to remain healthy. The accepted average now is 2354 calories per day, covering a range from 820 calories for a girl child less than one year old to 3500 for a boy of 16. The requirements for each country then have to be modified according to local conditions—the climate, the form in which the food is available, the size of the people and so on. Growing children and pregnant women need the most food and the most protein.

Contrary to popular belief, when the situation is assessed properly it turns out that India and Bangladesh are not the most desperately hungry countries. In terms of the *proportion* of the population that goes hungry or is actually starving, the West Indies and parts of Latin America and Africa (especially the Sahel) are far worse off. The average life expectancy at birth is 53 years for an Indian, higher than ever before, and higher, indeed, than that for a European aristocrat in the 19th century. In some parts of Africa, the life expectancy at birth is still below 30 years.

It is still commonly stated that 500 million people or more are starving in the world today. But official WHO figures suggest that about 10 million children under five are chronically undernourished, and even allowing each of these children five similarly malnourished adult relations this gives a total of 60 million in all, probably a much more accurate figure than the emotive 500 million. The number is still large, but it represents less than 2% of the world's population, a smaller proportion of undernourished than ever before.

North America? Best yields come when everything is right—good seed, the right amount of water at the right time, appropriate fertilizers, the right temperature. Average yields—the long-term trend—have boomed since the 1940s because of a vast increase in fertilizer use in the region, together with higher yielding varieties of seed. It is equally interesting that the variation from year to year, the fluctuations *about* the mean yield level, were much less in the 1950s and 1960s than in previous decades. Was this too a result of better technology, a triumph of man over nature? It now seems much more likely, as the vicissitudes of weather variability have returned to plague the farmers of the 1970s, that, in fact, there was less variability of yields from year to year in those bumper decades simply because the weather was less variable than it had been before and than it has now become again. High yields remain in prospect for the good years, but the weather still has a say in when the good years happen.

According to Professor Louis Thompson of Iowa State University, across the main grain growing states of the United States, weather variations account for well over 80 percent of the actual fluctuations in yields for wheat, corn and soya beans, and modern technology has not provided insurance against the vicissitudes of weather. Farther north in Canada grain production can be even more drastically affected by the weather, since at these higher latitudes late spring or early autumn frosts can cut back the length of the growing season to a critical extent. It is equally significant that the Soviet agricultural heartland is also very susceptible to weather changes, although there the limiting factor is mainly rainfall. Almost 99 percent of Soviet agricultural land has had an average rainfall below 28 inches (71 cm) per year in recent decades, whereas 60 percent of US agricultural land has had more rain than this in the good decades up to the 1970s. Only a small decline in rainfall is enough to cause a very bad harvest across much of the USSR—and even if twice as much rain falls in the next year, maintaining the average but with increased variability, it will be too late to save the lost food crops.

Thompson's studies of the corn and soya bean belts of the US led him to conclude that if the weather was as variable from now until the year 2000 as it was from

These pictures of the Kyzyl-Kum Desert region of Kazakhstan in the Soviet Union show how with good planning, good irrigation and good luck, desert areas can be made to blossom. But the balance is an artificial one, and precarious. If the water fails, the land will revert to desert in a few months.

Scrub-land on the edge of the Kyzyl-Kum.

Preparing the topsoil.

Irrigating newly planted cotton fields.

A successful rice-harvest.

1890 to 1955, then the average yield would be reduced by about three percent. That is alarming enough in itself, since we saw in Chapter 4 that a return to those weather conditions is exactly what we are experiencing. And although yields may still be increased by better technology and good farming practice, what Thompson is telling us is that we need a three percent increase even to stand still in terms of feeding the *present* world population—let alone the growing population of the real world. Far more disturbing even than this, however, is the implication that the three percent decline of food production will not be spread evenly over the years of the next two decades. Rather we can expect some years to be very good for grain production—as indeed 1978 was—while other years will be very bad—like 1976. This is a recipe for

A victim of famine in Biafra in 1970 with the distended stomach that characterizes severe malnutrition.

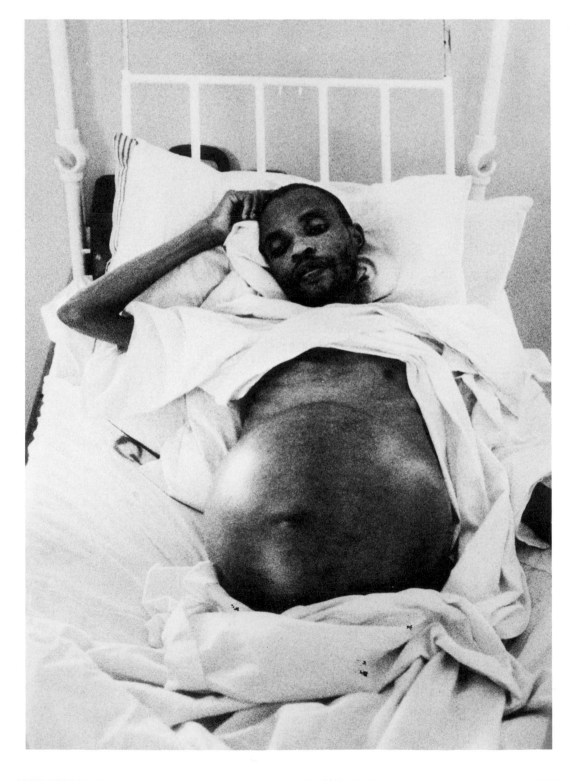

disaster. We must provide stockpiles in the good years if we are to have any hope of helping the hungry Third World ride out the bad years. Prudent levels of grain stocks —particularly when so much of the world today depends on the *surplus* produced by North America, the top few percent of the total yield—should be pitched high enough to take account of the returning pattern of increased climatic variation.

But the world as a whole could also do a great deal to reduce that dangerous dependence on North American surpluses— if we avoid the seductive trap of 'zero growth' and its implications.

The production and availability of food depends on four main factors: soil, climate, population and technology. These factors and the way they combine are affected by policies made at national, regional and international level. So food production is affected by politics in the broadest sense. Only about half of the immediately available suitable agricultural land is in use in any one year at present, partly because of political considerations such as the US 'land bank' policies. The consensus of expert opinion is that world food production could be doubled without any new technology to feed a population close to 8000 million at existing levels of nutrition. One estimate suggests that almost *20 times* that population (just under 160,000 million) could be fed if everyone made do with a basic 1967 'Japanese' diet—unexciting but sufficient to maintain life.

Even this is only part of the story. The *average* yield of rice per field in Bangladesh is only 15 percent of the yields obtained on experimental farms there, and if the 'best' modern farming practice were extended to all farms, the change would triple world production of wheat, quadruple production of maize, and increase rice production five-fold, according to American expert Professor Roger Revelle.

Without looking any further into speculation about the yields that *might* be achieved one day with techniques that still belong in the realms of science fiction, this is enough to show the overwhelming importance of economics and politics (both locally and internationally) in creating the knife-edge situation today, when only a small climatic nudge is enough to send the world slipping into a succession of food crises. Best farming

practices, technology and fertilizer cost money; all too often available resources in the most needy parts of the world are diverted into the acquisition of either armaments or imported Western technology.

At the same time the richest countries gobble up an ever bigger share of the global cake. In the 20 years up to 1970, while world production of cereals more than doubled, population increased by 50 percent —but that did not mean more food for all. More than half of the 'extra' food went to the richest third of the world's population. The 1000 million or so in the developed countries shared between them as much as the 2500+ million in the less developed countries. Just as the poorest people inside a country cannot buy enough food, so the poorest countries cannot buy a fair share on the *world* markets. Even the UK Government's Select Committee on Overseas Development acknowledged in a report in 1976 that 'the main answer to the world food problem is to give those who are hungry the means to feed themselves, or the income to buy food.'

This is not the place to look in detail at what might be involved, world-wide, in the radical change in attitudes such an analysis implies (I have dealt with the issues at length in my book *Future Worlds*). But one point deserves mention. The only way in which the poor countries can obtain the economic resources to buy or grow the food that they will need is by economic growth. The problem is basically one of poverty, and if poverty can be removed then the food problem will be largely solved. Far from 'zero growth' being a panacea for world problems, the greatest need today in poor countries is for balanced growth, at least for the next critical 50 years or so until they achieve decent living standards. Improved living standards have always gone hand in hand in the past with a declining birthrate. Enough growth in the right places will in theory automatically bring a levelling off in population, at a number well within the carrying capacity of planet Earth. Such a more truly global society will, however, still need to cope with the vagaries of the weather, making increasing use of the remarkable technological breakthroughs which are beginning today to give weathermen a picture of weather as a global force, not a local phenomenon.

In Senegal, a woman stands beside dead cattle in a once-fertile landscape.

THE SAHEL: A BELT OF STARVATION

During the early 1970s the public in many western nations became aware for the first time of the Sahel region. 'Sahel' is an Arabic word meaning shore, in this case the inland southern 'shore' of the Sahara, a zone stretching across Africa in which subsistence farming has, in past decades, been marginally possible. Since the 1930s, rainfall had been above average, and herdsmen and farmers had edged northwards. From 1973 onwards, that trend has reversed. Subsistence farmers and herdsmen have fled south as refugees. The land, over-used by men and cattle alike, is being reclaimed by the desert. Whole countries— Mali, Upper Volta, Niger, Chad—may become uninhabitable. No one knows whether the desiccation is part of an ebb and flow process that will reverse itself in the next decade, or whether it is part of a long-term trend which will make the Sahel a permanent desert. For the moment, at least, disaster has been contained. Aid has been shipped and flown into the stricken countries, and, despite the initial shocking death-toll of 100,000 or more, the 12 million made homeless by the changing climate have been saved from a worse catastrophe.

In Mauritania herdsmen try to save a drought victim.

Sahel farmers plant a crop on their dying land.

A refugee city near Nouakchott, Mauritania, which in 1978 housed 100,000 victims of the Sahel climatic disaster.

A woman and her baby in the refugees' shanty town.

In Chad, in 1973, refugees huddle under trees as a relief plane makes an air-drop.

US grain shipped in for the stricken.

GRAIN SORGHUM FURNISHED BY THE PEOPLE OF THE UNITED STATES OF AMERICA

CONTRACT KC-BP-2123

Grain piles up on the quayside.

An artificial stroke of
lightning – part of a
laboratory experiment to
further the scientific
understanding of
thunderstorms.

7: SCIENCE'S WEATHER EYES

We shall never be able to predict weather with absolute certainty. There are too many random factors for that. But by gathering ever more detailed information, by understanding the mechanisms of climate better, and by processing the results ever more rapidly, meteorologists should shortly be able to make forecasting almost as accurate as we can hope for.

Russian scientists near Moscow prepare to launch a flock of weather balloons, which will radio back information about conditions in the atmosphere's lower levels.

Weather is a global force and needs to be monitored on a global scale if it is ever to be properly understood and predicted. With this in mind 134 countries have joined together in an international organization, the World Meteorological Organization, to look at the problems of weather and its prediction. Under the auspices of the Geneva-based WMO, a project called the World Weather Watch (WWW) operates to train weather observers and ensure that both operators and instruments are available around the world to monitor the changing patterns of global weather.

Ten thousand meteorologists provide data for the WWW network, with thousands of volunteers on board ships adding crucial information from the oceans of the world. Satellites in orbit around the Earth help to provide an overview of the situation, and modern research aircraft flying into regions of particular interest help to sort out

the details where required. The computer network of the WMO links Washington, Moscow and Melbourne with a host of other lesser centers around the world; information from anywhere in the world can be plotted on weather charts and made available for study by meteorologists on the other side of the globe within a couple of hours. The WMO and its World Weather Watch provides one of the very few genuinely global activities of mankind.

As a science, meteorology's global monitoring system is becoming ever more complete and speedy. Weather satellites are no longer restricted to the observations made from space by their onboard instruments, but can relay information from ocean buoys and high-flying balloons back to a central computer. With all the problems outlined in previous chapters of this book, meteorology is fast becoming the most important science of all, with the hardware

A high altitude weather balloon is prepared for launching by scientists of the UK Meteorological Office.

to match. But it has taken a long time to reach this position.

Meteorology became an infant science in 1643 when Torricelli invented the barometer which made it possible to monitor changes in the pressure of the air at the Earth's surface from day to day. Within a few years thermometers too had been invented, giving us our first records of changing temperatures in absolute terms.

Daily weather records began to be gathered at sites across Europe almost immediately, and during the 1650s the first standardized instruments were issued by the Academia del Cimento in Florence, so that meteorologists could be sure that the measurements made at the different sites were using the same basic scales of measurement. Records of rainfall in Europe date back also to the 17th century; overall, the earliest instrument records combine to give a tantalizing glimpse in scientific terms of the severest phase of global climate since

the latest full Ice Age. But no real progress in understanding weather systems and making forecasts could occur until some means of rapid communication was developed. A weather forecast for Britain, for example, depends on knowledge of conditions to the west in the Atlantic. But in the 18th century the only way to get that information was by sailing ship—and the weather would move eastward faster than any ship.

True, the first weather map was drawn in 1820. But it was a historical document even then, drawn up from observations that had been made at 30 different sites 37 years previously. Meteorologists were beginning to understand weather patterns, but needed something much faster than the horse in order to get information in time to make useful forecasts.

Just two hundred years after the invention of the barometer, the invention of the electric telegraph in 1843 opened the way for the next step in the development of the science

A sand storm sweeping the Sudan in 1906 – the result of atmospheric changes that meterologists were already beginning to predict.

of meteorology. As soon as the cities of Europe were connected by telegraph, it became possible to make weather charts showing the broad essentials of local circulation patterns on the same day that the observations were made. In the early 20th century a new dimension—literally—was added to meteorological observation when French scientists began to make observations from balloons of how conditions changed with altitude above the ground. Meteorology finally came of age, however, when unmanned balloons carrying meteorological instruments and radio transmitters were developed in the 1930s.

These *radiosondes* provided a wealth of information about changing conditions in the atmosphere—and still do today. Monitoring their movements—first by optical telescopes, nowadays by radar—provides information about wind speed and direction at different altitudes, and the radio transmitters relay the standard information on temperature, pressure and humidity of the air. By the late 1940s it was possible to get a true picture of atmospheric circulation, linking the surface patterns with events above. Faster communications, more efficient instruments and high-speed computers have since combined to improve the view we have of the weather machine and our understanding of what makes it tick.

Twice a day at the same time all around the world (noon and midnight GMT), chosen stations of the WWW release their radiosondes into the atmosphere; merchant ships and aircraft add their contributions to the resulting flood of information, with news pouring in to the three main centers and 21 regional centers, where forecast charts are prepared on the basis of what amounts to an instantaneous snapshot of the present weather system, combined with information about how the patterns have been changing over the past few days. These regional charts are available for weather services of the different countries.

Some of the information from weather

WEATHER WAR

Waging war by modifying the weather was attempted by the US in Vietnam, but it is not a new idea. It goes back to 1850 when James Espy suggested to the US Congress a scheme to increase rainfall over the eastern United States by large-scale burning of forests in the western States, increasing convection and producing rainfall downwind, to the east.

Successful scientific rainmaking was first achieved in 1946 and 1947 by the addition of dry ice (solid CO_2) and silver iodide crystals to supercooled clouds (clouds below 0°C or 32°F); large-scale experiments carried out between 1948 and 1950 confirmed the possibility of achieving increased rainfall by cloud seeding, but for the past quarter century there has been very little practical development from these beginnings.

After repeated experiments with varying claims concerning the increase in rainfall produced by seeding, it now seems that any changes in rainfall produced by seeding are in general less than the statistical fluctuations occurring naturally, and very difficult to pin down. In the long term, a cloud-seeding project may increase local rainfall by 10–15 percent—not much, but enough to persuade the Americans to seed clouds over Southeast Asia during the Vietnam War from 1967 to 1972 in an attempt to disrupt deliveries of war materials from North Vietnam to the South.

A total of 2602 sorties were flown and 47,409 cannisters of seeding agent were injected into clouds over the five years. But evidence presented to the US Defense Department suggests that the results were minimal. The increase in rainfall during the monsoon never reached more than two or three inches above the normal 21 inches (53 cm). Apart from the fact that such a small variation is well within the range of the normal monsoon rainfall, an increase of only 10 percent in an already very wet season was not likely to have had any significant effect on the transportation along the Ho Chi Minh trail.

Though the practical effects were minimal, the political repercussions were not. What concerned most political objectors was, firstly, the fact that the operations were carried out in secret; and secondly the very notion—however impractical—was terrifying enough to inspire action. The abortive attempt to change Vietnam's climate led directly to the drafting of an international treaty on environmental warfare.

A CHECK-LIST OF EXTREMES

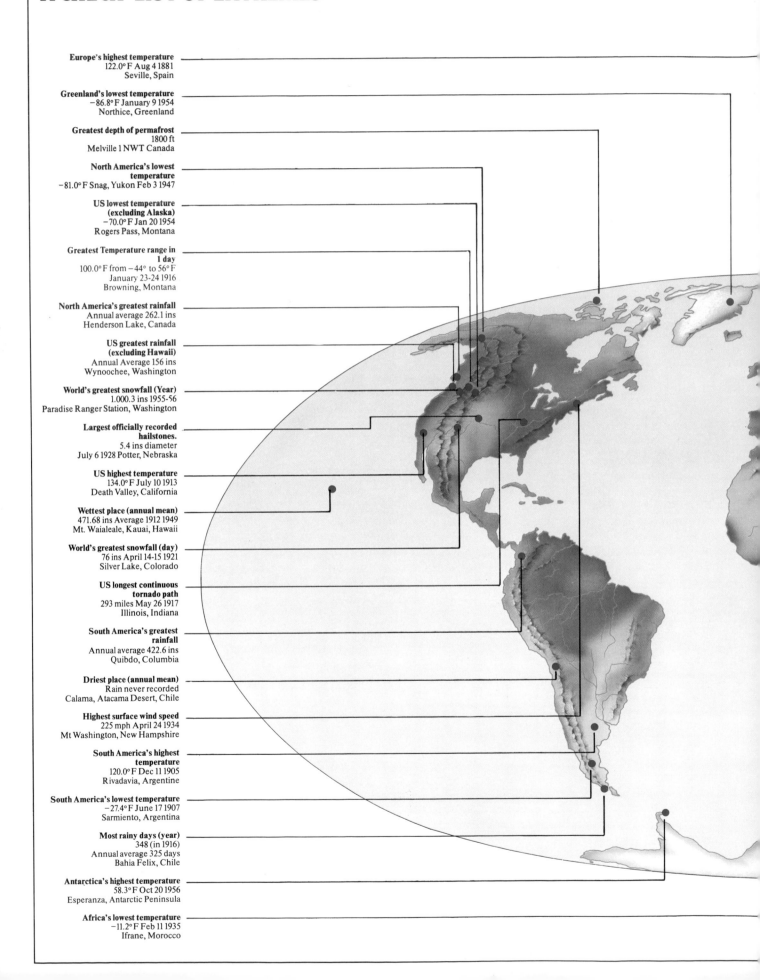

Europe's highest temperature
122.0°F Aug 4 1881
Seville, Spain

Greenland's lowest temperature
−86.8°F January 9 1954
Northice, Greenland

Greatest depth of permafrost
1800 ft
Melville 1 NWT Canada

North America's lowest temperature
−81.0°F Snag, Yukon Feb 3 1947

US lowest temperature (excluding Alaska)
−70.0°F Jan 20 1954
Rogers Pass, Montana

Greatest Temperature range in 1 day
100.0°F from −44° to 56°F
January 23-24 1916
Browning, Montana

North America's greatest rainfall
Annual average 262.1 ins
Henderson Lake, Canada

US greatest rainfall (excluding Hawaii)
Annual Average 156 ins
Wynoochee, Washington

World's greatest snowfall (Year)
1,000.3 ins 1955-56
Paradise Ranger Station, Washington

Largest officially recorded hailstones.
5.4 ins diameter
July 6 1928 Potter, Nebraska

US highest temperature
134.0°F July 10 1913
Death Valley, California

Wettest place (annual mean)
471.68 ins Average 1912 1949
Mt. Waialeale, Kauai, Hawaii

World's greatest snowfall (day)
76 ins April 14-15 1921
Silver Lake, Colorado

US longest continuous tornado path
293 miles May 26 1917
Illinois, Indiana

South America's greatest rainfall
Annual average 422.6 ins
Quibdo, Columbia

Driest place (annual mean)
Rain never recorded
Calama, Atacama Desert, Chile

Highest surface wind speed
225 mph April 24 1934
Mt Washington, New Hampshire

South America's highest temperature
120.0°F Dec 11 1905
Rivadavia, Argentine

South America's lowest temperature
−27.4°F June 17 1907
Sarmiento, Argentina

Most rainy days (year)
348 (in 1916)
Annual average 325 days
Bahia Felix, Chile

Antarctica's highest temperature
58.3°F Oct 20 1956
Esperanza, Antarctic Peninsula

Africa's lowest temperature
−11.2°F Feb 11 1935
Ifrane, Morocco

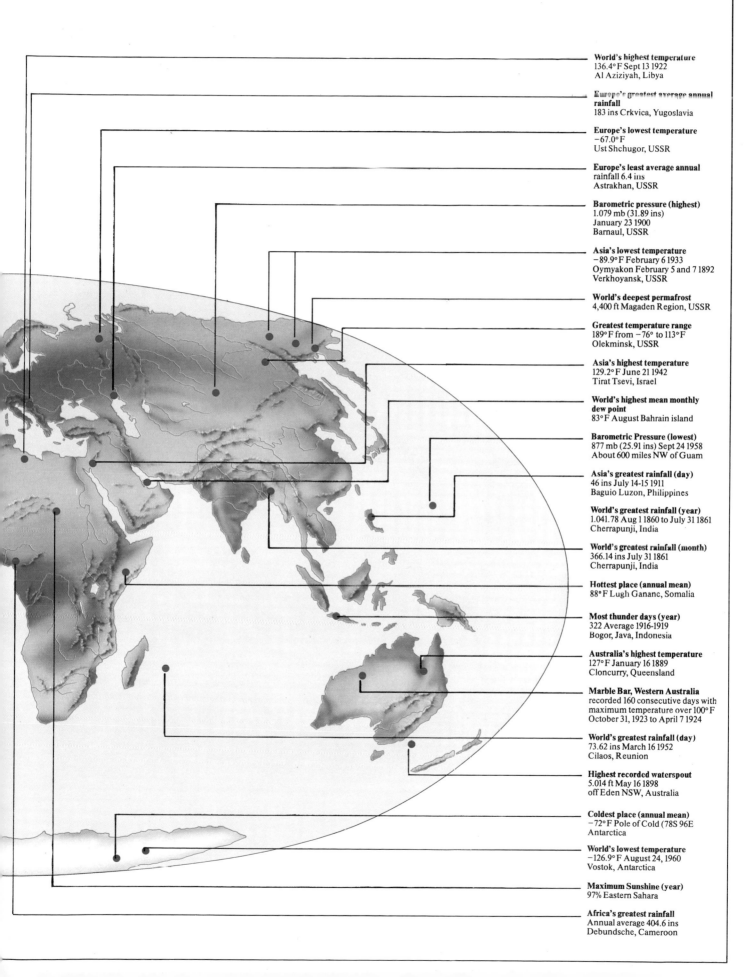

World's highest temperature
136.4°F Sept 13 1922
Al Aziziyah, Libya

Europe's greatest average annual rainfall
183 ins Crkvica, Yugoslavia

Europe's lowest temperature
−67.0°F
Ust Shchugor, USSR

Europe's least average annual
rainfall 6.4 ins
Astrakhan, USSR

Barometric pressure (highest)
1.079 mb (31.89 ins)
January 23 1900
Barnaul, USSR

Asia's lowest temperature
−89.9°F February 6 1933
Oymyakon February 5 and 7 1892
Verkhoyansk, USSR

World's deepest permafrost
4,400 ft Magaden Region, USSR

Greatest temperature range
189°F from −76° to 113°F
Olekminsk, USSR

Asia's highest temperature
129.2°F June 21 1942
Tirat Tsevi, Israel

World's highest mean monthly dew point
83°F August Bahrain island

Barometric Pressure (lowest)
877 mb (25.91 ins) Sept 24 1958
About 600 miles NW of Guam

Asia's greatest rainfall (day)
46 ins July 14-15 1911
Baguio Luzon, Philippines

World's greatest rainfall (year)
1.041.78 Aug 1 1860 to July 31 1861
Cherrapunji, India

World's greatest rainfall (month)
366.14 ins July 31 1861
Cherrapunji, India

Hottest place (annual mean)
88°F Lugh Gananc, Somalia

Most thunder days (year)
322 Average 1916-1919
Bogor, Java, Indonesia

Australia's highest temperature
127°F January 16 1889
Cloncurry, Queensland

Marble Bar, Western Australia
recorded 160 consecutive days with
maximum temperature over 100°F
October 31, 1923 to April 7 1924

World's greatest rainfall (day)
73.62 ins March 16 1952
Cilaos, Reunion

Highest recorded waterspout
5.014 ft May 16 1898
off Eden NSW, Australia

Coldest place (annual mean)
−72°F Pole of Cold (78S 96E
Antarctica

World's lowest temperature
−126.9°F August 24, 1960
Vostok, Antarctica

Maximum Sunshine (year)
97% Eastern Sahara

Africa's greatest rainfall
Annual average 404.6 ins
Debundsche, Cameroon

A Soviet weather satellite, solar panels extended, on display in Moscow.

A Soviet scientist adjusts the antennae used to receive signals from weather satellites.

satellites is even more readily available to anyone with sufficient funds and some electronic knowledge who chooses to build a suitable antenna and receiving system. Many schools pull in their own weather pictures from the satellites passing overhead—not the best pictures that the high-quality links with sophisticated ground stations provide, but sufficient to show cloud cover and the swirling local weather patterns, and to make their own local forecasts.

Two kinds of weather satellite are now in common use. Most orbit over the poles, with the Earth rotating underneath them, so that on successive passes around the globe the satellite builds up a picture of the entire global weather pattern. Others, becoming increasingly important, are in the so-called 'geostationary' orbits, orbiting once in 24 hours so that they appear to hang over one region of the globe, itself turning once in 24 hours. These give permanent coverage of a region, such as Europe. Some satellites extend their coverage over the nighttime part of the Earth using infrared sensors, and as they become increasingly sophisticated they may one day replace radiosondes; as yet, however, nothing can match the detailed coverage provided by balloon-borne instruments, and old and new work hand in hand.

This vast wealth of information would, however, be of little use without the high speed computers which can assimilate the data and release it out in an easily understood form in a matter of hours. The idea behind a numerical 'model' of the atmosphere is simple enough. If we know the pressure, temperature and windspeed at enough points throughout the atmosphere, then we should be able to predict how things are going to develop from the present position, obtaining an infallible weather forecast. Of course we would have to include numbers to take account of the heating effect of the Sun, the rotation of the Earth, and the influence of the oceans. But it could be done—in principle.

The difficulty is that one needs many numbers covering a fine mesh grid over the Earth—and in depth in layers through the atmosphere—to have any hope of a successful forecast. This first problem was overcome with the development of computers big enough to handle the numbers. But then the computer forecasters hit another snag—

their machines were in some cases giving reasonable forecasts for 12 hours or so ahead. But they were taking much longer than 12 hours to produce the 'forecasts,' since it took so long to process the numbers! By the time the forecast appeared, the much more rapid workings of the real atmosphere had overtaken the computer.

Now this problem too has been solved. At least modern computers get the forecasts out in time for them to be useful. But there is still a long way to go before the forecasts are as accurate and reliable as we would like.

As things stand now, information from the scattered observers of the WWW pours into the computers of a major center, such as that of the UK Meteorological Office in Bracknell, in the hours immediately after midnight and noon GMT. The fastest computers—the ones at Bracknell are just about the best—then produce a 24-hour forecast from the raw data in a few minutes and continue to give a longer range forecast for the three days ahead, all well within an hour; having sketched in the broad picture, the machines then turn to filling in details for local regions where much more data may be available and there may be considerably more people to be interested in the weather—Western Europe and Britain in

The Soviet M-20 computer at Moscow's Central Weather Forecast Bureau, which is used to synthesize information from scores of weather satellites and continuously update forecasts for the Soviet Union.

the case of the Bracknell predictions. The computer forecasts are not, however, taken as gospel even by the people who work with the machines. Human experience and judgment of how weather systems will develop, and especially local knowledge, are used to color the cold facts of the computer forecast somewhat, shading in a little more detail

still and turning the numbers into a forecast in words for the benefit of ordinary people watching television or reading the forecast in their newspapers.

With all of this modern technology plus the benefit of human experience, the forecasts are still not perfect, and there are good reasons to believe that in the literal sense

These two satellite shots show the variety of information that can be derived from false color photography.
Below, a view of Hurricane Katrina in September 1975 shows the hot (blue) central column with cooler areas to the sides and in the eye. At bottom, is a Nimbus-5 weather satellite map of the distribution of moisture over the Earth in an average January. The light blue areas are humid, the darker areas, progressively drier. The green areas are extremely dry. Ground temperatures stand out similarly dramatically – the effects of the southern hemisphere summer are picked out in red. Previously, such information would take weeks to assemble – too long to be of use.

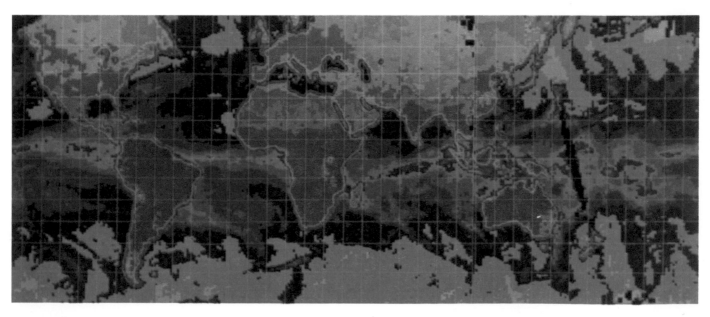

A weather satellite radio-receiver.

A rain recorder.

Preparing a weather chart.

A completed chart.

of the word they never can be perfect. The extent of the WWW's network of observing stations is vast, but still leaves large gaps, regions where very little accurate weather data is available to be fed into the computers. So the programs have to be made to guess reasonable numbers to put into the gaps—extrapolating from the conditions in next-door regions from which numbers are available. This problem can be reduced by a massive increase in meteorological observing sites or by the (probably equally expensive) development of much more accurate systems of monitoring weather from satellites. But the cost becomes harder and harder to justify the closer we get to perfection—improving the accuracy of forecasts from 80 percent to 90 percent probably costs as much again as the original 80 percent

forecast itself, while improving further from 90 percent to 95 percent costs as much as the 90 percent forecast, with a further doubling of costs for each halving of the gap between present accuracy and 100 percent.

There is also a fundamental 'cut off' to the accuracy of forecasts, brought about because the weather machine of our planet is not running in accordance with precisely predictable rules. There is a random element built in to the whole apparatus, so that (to take a very simple example) the precise moment when a raindrop falls is determined not just by physical conditions but to a small extent by chance. Adding up all these little chance variations over the whole system produces a kind of background 'noise,' a blurring around the edges of the numerical

WEATHER MODIFICATION-WHO PAYS?

Weather modification, even if successful, cannot be contained within the borders of one farm or, often, one country. Clouds seeded over one country may rain somewhere else—perhaps causing floods and damaging crops. Or successful seeding may bring complaints from states 'downwind' that insufficient water has been left for *their* crops! As things stand today, the onus is on the claimant to prove that weather modification has caused the damage. But as weather modification becomes more reliable, the situation may change. Some countries are already arguing that the burden of proof should lie on the weather modifier, to prove that the modification was harmless (a healthy development anyway, in that it encourages caution in tinkering with the forces of nature).

The spirit of this argument is summed up in a memorandum from the Canadian Legal Division of the Department of External Affairs, in 1969: 'under international law every State has a duty to prevent, as far as possible, its own nationals and foreign nationals within its territory from committing injurious acts against other States. A State which does not comply with this duty, either intentionally or maliciously or through culpable negligence is guilty of an international offense for which it has to bear

original responsibility. However, it is of course in practice impossible for a State to prevent all injurious acts which a private person might commit against a foreign State. It is for that reason that a State must, according to international law, bear vicarious responsibility for such injurious acts of private individuals as it is unable to prevent.'

That pretty clearly makes a state liable for activities even of private weather modifiers within its territory, if indeed they cause damage to another state. Legally, it seems, the state where the seeding takes place is responsible for any damage outside its borders.

But what about individuals *within* a state, harmed by the weather modification activities of government agencies? The recent drought in California broke after more than two years with devastating floods—just at a time when cloud seeding experiments were being undertaken in desperation. Many of the flood victims blamed the government for making the situation worse than it might otherwise have been through the seeding; the processes of law grind slow, and it remains to be seen whether such will be proved to be the case. But the precedents are all in favor of the government.

In December 1955 north and central

calculations, which means that we will never be able to forecast *exactly* how the weather will develop. Small scale phenomena, such as thunderstorms, literally cannot be predicted more than a few hours ahead, while even the larger features of the wiggling jet stream and associated depressions of the circumpolar vortex are not predictable more than five days ahead.

In practice this means that scientists can take a three day forecast and update it every 12 hours with new data from the real world, so that we can always keep our forecasts three days in advance of the global weather machine. But we will never do much better than that.

There have been attempts to provide monthly forecasts, predicting broad features of the weather 30 days ahead, most notably from the UK Meteorological Office team. But their success rate with these forecasts has been far from good. One can achieve as much success without aid from expensive electronic computers simply by remembering where the weather systems come from at one's latitude (from the west in the case of Europe and North America); thus, by and large, conditions 'upstream' will be coming your way in the weeks ahead. Watch for the wiggles in the jet, and when a blocking high gets established change the 'forecast' to assume that things will stay much as they are for the immediate future. Between the two, with a little practice, you can soon astonish your friends and get a reputation as a weather prophet.

Curiously, though, when we look even further ahead, well beyond a month or so,

---

California also suffered devastating storms, covering 100,000 square miles (259,000 sq km), 60 percent of the area of the State. Many areas were flooded, with direct financial losses exceeding $200 million and 64 lives lost. Yuba City, lying where the Yuba and Feather Rivers meet, was hardest hit of all, when a levee system collapsed. Here alone, 37 people died, 3277 were injured, 467 homes destroyed and 5745 damaged. In spite of legal advice that they had little chance of success, several of the 'injured parties' went to court seeking damages against the State of California, Pacific Gas and Electric Company and North American Weather Consultants, who had been jointly involved in cloud seeding activities in the 1955–56 season. The suit was filed in September 1958, including the key allegation that 'collapse and breaking of the levees was proximately caused or contributed to by the negligent maintenance and operation of rain-making equipment, and together with the escaping waters proximately resulted in damage to plaintiffs.'

There were some nice legal touches about the case, not least the fact that by suing the State government the plaintiffs were in effect suing themselves, since the government is supposed to be the instrument of the people. With such subtle arguments and the need for expert witnesses on either side to present their evidence and opinions, pre-trial proceedings took five years, and the case came to court in 1963. Frustratingly for would-be weather litigants today, as in so many complicated legal cases, a deal was done between the defendants and plaintiffs before the judge reached his decision. The weather modification action was, in effect, withdrawn because of a stronger case against the State for the failure of the levee system; the plaintiffs had agreed not to appeal if they lost the case against Pacific Gas and Electric and North America Weather Consultants, in exchange for which the defendants agreed to pay the plaintiffs' fees—an arrangement known as 'buying an appeal.'

The weather modification issue could therefore remain in abeyance. Judge Mac-Murray in April 1964: 'Plaintiffs may not recover against the Pacific Gas and Electric Company or North American Weather Consultants as they have failed in the burden of proof. . . . The breaking of the levees was neither proximately caused nor contributed to either by the maintenance or by the operation of the artificial rainmaking equipment of any defendant in this lawsuit.'

The judge did, however, find against the State concerning its responsibility for the levee system which failed, and the plaintiffs won a total of $6.3 million in damages—almost ten years after the disaster.

The deal not to conduct an appeal on the weather modification case leaves the issue still legally open, but is hardly encouraging for any Californians wondering what to do in the wake of the latest disaster. Some day, though, a plaintiff is going to argue convincingly that damage was caused by the weather modifiers. It should be quite a case.

forecasting becomes again more reliable in a different sense. It is in this area of seasonal forecasting that the future of weather forecasting offers the most exciting prospects for the next few years.

For such extended forecasts, the little details of the background 'noise' tend to average out. We cannot say six months in advance that 6 September will be a sunny day. But we *can* say, by late spring, whether the autumn of the same year is likely to be wet or dry, cold or mild. At least we can do this with some confidence for some regions of the globe. In the years ahead scientists hope to extend this skill to more and more of the regions of the globe, and to make seasonal forecasts publicly available.

In a nutshell the technique depends on the close relationship between ocean temperatures and atmospheric circulation, and on the way the ocean 'remembers' temperature patterns from one season to another. Areas of warm and cold water affect the atmosphere above, and in the latitudes of the North Pacific and North Atlantic their influence decides just where and by how much, the jet stream swings north and south on its zigzag path around the globe. Sweeping warm air north, or cold air south, the zigzagging jet may reinforce the temperature differences of nearby patches of ocean, building in a pattern that does not change rapidly, compared with the day-to-day fluctuations of weather that are the

concern of our ordinary forecasts.

With Pacific waters north of Hawaii cold, for example, and warmer waters near the western seaboard of the US, the jet will swing south around the cold patch, north again across the warmer water and then east across the continent—conditions for a brisk, cold winter (though not on the scale of 1977 or 1978) which can be seen coming months in advance by monitoring the ocean temperatures. A reversed pattern of warm and cold in the Pacific gives a jet sweeping first north across warm water then south around cooler water and into California before turning to the northeast across the continent—a reliable recipe for warm winters in the eastern States and cold (by their standards) winters in the southwest.

For Britain and Europe the key patch of ocean lies south of Newfoundland, which sets the jet swinging in favor of mild or cold winters across the Atlantic. The details of all these effects are only now being worked out. Apart from their practical value, however, they are especially interesting because they depend on exactly the opposite philosophical approach from that of the hard line computer forecasters. With a computer all one needs are the numbers from the WWW to make a forecast; watching the swinging jet stream and warm and cold regions of ocean, the forecast depends entirely on viewing the physical reality of the whole weather machine. One technique

Left: The instrument panel of a meteorological office in San Diego, California.

A set of Chinese stamps commemorate advances in Chinese meteorology: weather balloons, radio-links, anti-hail rockets and the preparation of charts.

One of the stranger aspects of weather control – Soviet techniques for preventing hailstorms. At right, a team of anti-hail gunners in the Fergana Valley, Uzbekhistan, prepare to protect local cotton fields. The shells are filled with chemical agents that scatter in the clouds providing microscopic cores, to which moisture droplets cling and fall as miniature hailstones that melt before they land.

Anti-hail rockets in Moldavia.

Launch of an anti-hail rocket in the Alazan Valley, Georgia.

is like counting the trees in the forest while the other is like photographing the wood from above to determine its overall shape. And the best results of all, of course, come when the two techniques are combined, as when the skillful human meteorologist modifies a computer forecast in the light of a lifetimes' experience of the weather.

So there are real prospects that the weather will be understood and predicted to the benefit of farmers and all of us to an unprecedented degree of accuracy by the end of the present century. The age-old dream of *controlling* the weather is still a long way off. But already weather control exists in its infancy. The Soviet Union prevents hail damage to crops by encouraging the storm clouds to produce rain instead of hail. This has involved techniques ranging from 'seeding' the clouds with crystals dropped by aircraft to bombarding the clouds with barrages from anti-aircraft guns—a rare case of weapons being turned to beneficial peacetime use.

The most promising developments in modifying the force of the weather, however, now seem to be efforts aimed at tempering the force of hurricanes so that their life-giving rain can fall without bringing destruction in its wake.

Hurricane modification depends on cloud seeding—supplying suitable crystals which encourage the condensation of water nuclei, which in turn grow into raindrops. When the temperature in a cloud falls below 32°F (0°C) it contains a mixture of 'supercooled' water droplets and ice crystals. Because vapor pressure over the droplets is greater than over the ice, the liquid drops evaporate while water condenses on to the ice crystals and freezes. Eventually ice crystals become large enough to fall towards the ground, either arriving as snow or melting into rain *en route*. But this entire process, it is thought, depends on the presence of condensation nuclei on which the initial ice crystals can grow. These nuclei may come from wind-blown dust or plant material; but whatever the source it seems they are essential for this rainfall process to operate. Clouds containing no such nuclei can cool to as much as –4°F (–20°C) without droplets freezing, and therefore without any precipitation. Addition of particles of solid material—dry ice, sodium iodide or others—to such clouds can in principle initiate the rainfall mechanism by providing the nuclei on which ice crystals begin to grow. Successful seeding produces a release of latent heat as water vapor is converted into liquid, and this heat causes air to expand, affecting convection and wind speeds inside the hurricane. One idea now being tested in America is that seeding might be used to persuade a fierce hurricane into settling into a much calmer state.

In a strong hurricane the 'eye' around which the spinning winds rotate may be only about 15 miles (24 km) across. This is dominated by the high banked clouds and spinning winds of the eyewall. But if the eye could be expanded to, say, 30 miles (48 km) across, then the spinning winds

would move that much slower and their damaging effects would be reduced without stopping the rain that countries like Mexico need. The idea is simple—to 'seed' the clouds in a ring outside the eyewall so that these outer clouds grow, towering higher even than the eyewall as convection does its work. These new clouds and convection systems would then dominate the hurricane; the old eyewall would dissipate and a new, larger eye would become established.

So much, at least, is the theory. It has yet to be accepted as established practice, but tests have already been carried out to see what happens. Hurricane modification was first attempted in an isolated case in 1947 when a seeded hurricane changed course and

Cloud-seeding in Australia: a canister of silver iodide is prepared (below), and at right, rain begins to fall after release of the chemical. It remains arguable, however, whether seeding actually causes rain, or whether the rain would have fallen anyway.

caused extensive damage in Georgia, USA. No one accepted blame for the damage, but the result discouraged hurricane seeding experiments until Project Stormfury, which began in 1960 and ran for 14 years. Several hurricanes were seeded, with inconclusive results. Some seeded hurricanes apparently grew fiercer, some weakened, some changed direction, and some did not change at all.

A completely different approach to hurricane modification was suggested by an American team in 1975, who pointed out that another way of adding to the input of heat to a convective system would be to spread black material—soot—across the clouds. Their idea was to make smoke by modifying the afterburners of the engines of a B-52 bomber and spread smutty trails across the sky. As with conventional seeding, the introduction of a source of energy in this way could, in principle, be used to disrupt the structure of a hurricane—or, equally, to enhance the development of a hurricane and increase its potential for destruction. As before, if convection outside the eyewall is stimulated the hurricane should weaken, while if convection inside the eyewall is stimulated the hurricane

The effects of cloud seeding: *Right:* The collapse of two cloud layers as a result of condensation a few minutes after seeding, during Project Cirrus, an early attempt at weather modification over New York in 1948.

Below: A sequence of four shots showing the growth of rain-cloud from a 23,000-foot (7000-meter) cumulus layer to a 29,000-foot (9000-meter) thunderhead. After this experiment over Australia, the thunderhead reached 40,000 feet (12,000 meters) and rain fell for two and a half hours.

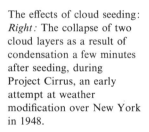

should gain in strength. While there are also the potential advantages in diverting ordinary storm systems into dry regions such as the western US and intensifying them by such means, sufficient stimulation might perhaps cause damaging floods.

The dangers of such experiments notwithstanding, such ideas are exciting. From all that we have seen of the evidence gathered in this book, there can be no doubt that the world is heading into stormier weather, with harsher conditions for agriculture. Though the world's population is still rising and reserves of food are likely to be low, we *can* cope (looking at the problem purely in scientific and technological terms), if we work together on a global scale to overcome these problems. Within a hundred years we could see a peaceful, well-fed world in which weather is beginning to be bent to man's will for productive purposes. If our co-operation or political inventiveness fails, however, then international conflict will be increasingly likely; then we may see the other side of the coin—weather forces harnessed for destruction. In any event, the world's climate over the next few decades will be of consuming interest.

BOLTS FROM HEAVEN

A flash of lightning is one of nature's most awesome spectacles. Such sudden and often destructive releases of energy have generated myths and folktales in every culture. In ancient Greece, it was Zeus, the king of the Gods, who dealt out 'thunderbolts.' Even in the West, a lightning strike is termed by insurers an 'act of God.'

Since 1749, when the American scientist Benjamin Franklin showed that lightning was a giant electric spark by allowing a key attached to a kite to act as a lightning conductor, scientists have established a more rational approach (though the details are still far from clear). In a thundercloud, electrical charges are created as droplets of moisture coalesce and air masses flow. The electrical difference between one pocket of air and another (or the ground) builds until a small 'leader' stroke opens an electrical pathway for the massive 'return stroke,' a tremendous release of energy that may amount to a hundred million volts. Most discharges occur in clouds, and no more than 40 percent strike the ground. Whether it reaches the ground or not, lightning causes thunder: the flash heats the air, which expands, producing waves identical to those of sound.

At any one time, there are some 1800 thunderstorms active worldwide, producing 150 discharges per second. Not surprisingly, tall buildings may be struck a hundred times annually; and every year scores of people and unknown numbers of animals are killed by lightning.

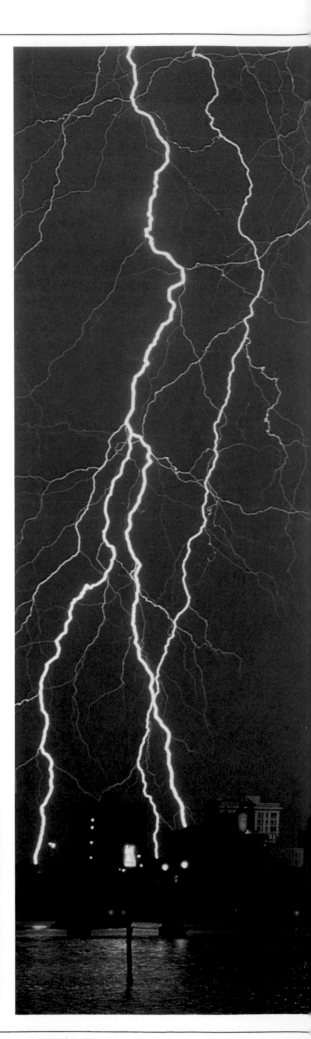

A single bolt strikes in the Place des Armes, Quebec.

Multiple strikes over Tampa, Florida.

A portable lightning
conductor: this early
19th-century device was
inspired by current research
into the electrical nature
of lightning. In fact, the
chances of any individual
being struck are so remote
that it scarcely seems
worth the trouble.

During his historic
experiment establishing
the electrical nature of
lightning, Benjamin Franklin
holds a kite to pick up a
charge, and watches a spark
leap from a key attached
to the line.

Lightning conductors *à la môde* in Paris, 1778.

A Swedish scientist, Engelstad, dies repeating Franklin's experiment, 1909.

One of the most
extraordinary and
controversial of phenomena
is that of ball lightning.
There have been a number
of accounts of incandescent
balls up to a foot (30 cm)
across, floating slowly
across rooftops, or even, on
rare occasions, entering
rooms. Sometimes they
disappear in a flash. Such
incidents have been widely
dismissed by scientists
because there is as yet
no theory that can account
for such events.

This picture, taken at
Castleford, Yorkshire,
in 1961, is the only known
photograph of ball lightning
(if that, indeed, is what
it is). The photographer,
Roy Jennings, opened his
shutter and recorded the
progress of the ball over
roof tops until it exploded.

The two drawings at
right record the reported
path of ball lightning which
floated into a hotel room
in the Gorges du Loup,
near Nice, France. The ball
was 8 inches (20 cm) in
diameter. According to
eyewitness reports, it
drifted round the room, and
then floated back out of the
window to explode near
a bridge.

A flock of 504 sheep killed by a bolt of lightning in July, 1918 in Wasatch National Forest, Utah. Although the path of lightning is less than an inch (2.5 cm) across, its effects spread in the ground.

Left: The effect of a lightning strike on a church.

Right: An isolated oak tree shattered by lightning, which usually follows the best conducting path, the moist layer below the bark.

A brilliant return-stroke lights up a lakeside landscape.

ACKNOWLEDGEMENTS

front cover Colour Library International
back cover, 82 Maisal Photochrome Inc/
  N W Ekla
title page Frank W Lane
contents page NOAA
6–7 Photo Researchers Inc/
  Tom McHugh
8–9 *top* Keystone Press Agency
8–9 *bottom* Rex Features
10 Keystone Press Agency
11 Novosti Press Agency
12–13, 14, 15 *top, center and bottom*, 16
  Keystone Press Agency
18 John Hillelson Agency
19, 20, 21 *top* Stephen F Morley
21 *bottom* Keystone Press Agency
22–3 NOAA
24 *top* Stephen F Morley
24 *bottom*, 25 Keystone Press Agency
26–7 NASA
28–9 Aerofilms
30–1 NOAA
33 Jim Marks
34–5 Radio Times Hulton Picture Library
36, 37 Nigel Osborne
38 Picturepoint
39, 40 *top* NASA
40 *bottom* Laurence Bradbury
41 *top* Nigel Osborne
41 *bottom*, 43 Laurence Bradbury
44 *top, center and bottom* NASA
45 Gary Hinks
46 Laurence Bradbury
47 Radio Times Hulton Picture Library
  and *'Snowcrystals' (McGraw Hill)
48, 49 NASA
50–1, 51 *inset* Aerofilms
52 Tony Morrison
52 *top right* RIDA/R T J Moody
52 *top center and bottom center right* The
  MacQuitty International Collection
52 *bottom right* RIDA/R Towse
53 RIDA/Alex Maltman
54–5 Aerofilms
55 *inset* Rex Features
56–7 Frank W Lane
58–9 Mary Evans Picture Library
60 *top and bottom* Radio Times Hulton
  Picture Library
61 *top left, top right and bottom* Camera
  Press/Gus Coral
62 *top* Frank W Lane/ American Red
  Cross
62 *bottom* Camera Press/US Army Corps
  of Engineers
63 Frank W Lane
64 Colorific!/Gianni Tortoli
65 *top and bottom* Popperfoto
68 *left*, 68–9, 69 *inset* Radio Times
  Hulton Picture Library
71 Camera Press/Thomas D Stevens
  (The Providence Journal Bulletin)
72 *bottom*, 73 *bottom* Rex Features

72 *top*, 73 *top* Radio Times Hulton
  Picture Library
74, 76 Frank W Lane
78–9 J. Allan Cash
80 Mary Evans Picture Library
81 *top* Frank W Lane
81 *bottom* Radio Times Hulton Picture
  Library
82 *Maisal Photochrome Inc/ N W Ekla
83 * Blake Allison
84, 85 Frank W Lane
86 Photo Researchers Inc/Margaret
  Durrance
87 *M P Garrod
88–9, 89 *top* Frank W Lane
90–1 Reproduced by courtesy of the
  Trustees, The National Gallery,
  London
92 *Peterborough Psalter/Listener
94 *top and bottom*, 95 *top, center and
  bottom* Jonathan Morse
96, 97 *Swiss National Tourist Office
98 *top, center and bottom*, 99 Radio
  Times Hulton Picture Library
100, 101 Oxford Scientific Films/
  L L T Rhodes
102 Radio Times Hulton Picture Library
103 Crown Copyright/Ministry of
  Defence Photo
106, 107, 108, 109 *top* Radio Times
  Hulton Picture Library
109 *bottom* Keystone Press Agency
110–11 Institute of Geological Sciences
113 *top and bottom* Laurence Bradbury
114–15 Gary Hinks
116, 117 Laurence Bradbury
118–19 RIDA/R C L Wilson
121 Sygma
122 Laurence Bradbury
123 *top and center* Institute of Geological
  Sciences
123 *bottom* RIDA/D Rolls
124 supplied by the Meteorological
  Office, Bracknell
126 Institute of Geological Sciences
127 Oxford Museum
128–9 Camera Press/US Navy
130 *top*, 130–1, 131 *top* York Museum/
  Temple Anderson Collection
132–3 Frank W Lane
134–5 John Hillelson Agency
136, 137, 138–9 Keystone Press Agency
141, 142–3, 143 *inset* Rex Features
146 *top, center and bottom*, 147 Novosti
  Press Agency
148 Rex Features
150–1, 152–3 John Hillelson Agency
156 *top* Alan Hutchinson Library
156 *bottom*, 157 Keystone Press Agency
158–9 Photo Researchers Inc
160 Novosti Press Agency
161 *G A Robinson
162 Radio Times Hulton Picture Library
164–5 Jim Marks
166 *top and bottom*, 167 Novosti Press
  Agency
168 *top* NOAA/The Californian Institute

of Earth Planetary and Life Sciences
168 *bottom* NASA
169 *top left* supplied by the
  Meteorological Office, Bracknell
169 *center left* *Crown Copyright
169 *top and bottom right* *Crown
  Copyright
169 *center right* 'Weather Business'
  (Aldus Books)
172 *top* Daily Telegraph Colour Library/
  L L T Rhodes
174, 175 *top and bottom* Novosti Press
  Agency
176, 177 The Australian Information
  Servicé, London
178 *bottom left and right* *CSIRO,
  Sydney
178 *top*, 179 *top* *US Army, Navy, Air
  Force General Electric Equipment
179 *bottom left and right* *CSIRO,
  Sudnay
180, 181 Photo Researchers Inc
182 *left*, 182–3, 183 *top right and bottom
  right*, 184 *inset*, 185 *inset* Mary Evans
  Picture Library
184–5 Frank W Lane/Roy Jennings
186–7 Frank W Lane/US Forest Service
186 *inset* Photo Researchers Inc.
187 *inset* Frank W Lane
188–9 Camera Press

*pictures supplied by the Meteorological
  Office, Bracknell
Picture Research—Susan de la Plain
          Tim Fraser

INDEX